The Right Way to Eat Spaghetti

by Bob and Marilyn Donahue

Tyndale House Publishers, Inc.
Wheaton, Illinois

Photo and art credits: Bill Bilsley—front cover, p. 43; Ken Westphal—pp. 8, 72-73; Jonathan A. Meyers—p. 9; Jim Steere—pp. 12-13, 25, 67; Warren Ludwig—pp. 15, 34; Paul Buddle—p. 29; Michael Goldberg—p. 32; Rubberstampede—pp. 35, 46, 62; Frank Bussy—pp. 40-41; Bob Taylor—pp. 45, 51; John Hayes—pp. 58, 59; Ed Carlin—p. 61; Paul Pavlik—p. 65; Jim Whitmer—p. 75; Steve Takatsuno—p. 83; Michael Chickey—p. 90.

First printing, December 1987

Library of Congress Catalog Card Number 87-51137
ISBN 0-8423-5597-9
Copyright 1987 by Bob and Marilyn Donahue
All rights reserved
Printed in the United States of America

CONTENTS

INTRODUCTION
Meet Ned the Nerd 7

CHAPTER ONE
Take a Good Look at Yourself 11

CHAPTER TWO
Let's Shake on It 19

CHAPTER THREE
Chitchat 27

CHAPTER FOUR
Tools of the Trade 37

CHAPER FIVE
Let's Party! 49

CHAPTER SIX
Out on the Town 57

CHAPTER SEVEN
Be My Guest 65

CHAPTER EIGHT
Don't Call Me—I'll Call You 71

CHAPTER NINE
On the Job 79

CHAPTER TEN
Mail Call 85

CONCLUSION
Manners That Matter—
and a Few That Don't 93

INTRODUCTION

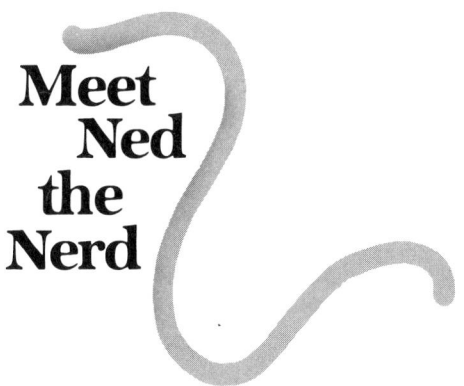

Meet Ned the Nerd

Ned the Nerd is a Nearth kid. This means that he lives on a small K-type planet called Nearth. Some mornings the sun comes up in the west, as it should, and sets in the east at night. But occasionally it doesn't bother to appear for days at a time. When this happens, people walk around in the dark and stumble a lot.

The planet Nearth has a few other problems. For one thing, gravity is iffy. When Ned pours himself a glass of milk, the milk might fall into the glass or take off sideways across the room. When he sips his soup, he tries to do it carefully, but he often makes a wet, slurpy sound and the soup slides across his T-shirt and onto the tablecloth.

No matter how hard Ned tries to look nice when he goes outside, he can never keep his hair combed or his clothes straight because the weather on Nearth is so unpredictable. It can rain or snow at any time, even without clouds, and the wind blows in all directions, including up and down.

When Ned meets a new Nearthling, his problems begin all over again. He knows all about shaking hands, but can never remember which one to use. To add to his other problems, Ned is all thumbs.

Yes, Ned has a tough life and things aren't getting any

easier. On Nearth the rules of nature have shorted out, and there is no order.

"When you live in a place like this," Ned says, "you never know what to expect. No matter how hard you try to do things right, you always goof up."

Do you ever feel like a Nearthling? Do you have the best intentions, but always mess up? Cheer up! You're on the planet Earth, and all systems are A-OK. The sun's path across the sky follows a regular pattern. The weather is predictable, at least most of the time. When you throw a ball into the air, it will come down. You can depend on it!

This orderly system of natural rules makes your life easier. It lets you know what to expect. It helps you know how to react.

Just as you need to have order in the world around you, you need to have order in your relationships with other people. Many people call this kind of order **good manners.**

The fancy word for good manners is **etiquette.** All etiquette really means is

*knowing when to do something, knowing the best way to do it, and
knowing when you shouldn't do it at all.*

Years ago kids were expected to memorize long lists of social dos and don'ts. Goofing up in public was considered a disgrace, and making a **faux pas*** was enough to ruin a kid's week.

Some old-fashioned rules of so-

*A **faux pas** (pronounced foe-paw) is a #1 goof.

8 The Right Way to Eat Spaghetti

cial behavior seem pretty funny today:

—*Never sit at the table in your shirt sleeves.*
—*Never whistle in public.*
—*Don't eat fruit on a public street.*
—*Don't use slang.*
—*Never say, "Yeah."*
—*Don't pick up any food with your fingers.*

Times have changed, but the ways people look and act are still important. Fortunately, no one expects you to memorize a long list of etiquette rules. All you have to do is understand what good manners really mean.

Ned the Nerd didn't have much of a chance in his goofy world, but things can be different for you. Don't wait another second. Keep turning the pages of this book and see how much fun it is to become an expert on manners that matter.

If you're sloppy and you're floppy
And you feel just like a nerd,
Or you want to sound so brilliant
But you just can't find the words—
If you hate those introductions
And can't write thank-you notes,
Or you come to the lunch table
And you eat just like a goat—
If you want to look outstanding
When you're headin' on a date,
But some stumblin' and a-mumblin'
Are the outcomes of your fate—
Don't you panic! Don't give up!
You can be a great success;
Learn which manners really matter—
And don't settle, no, for less!

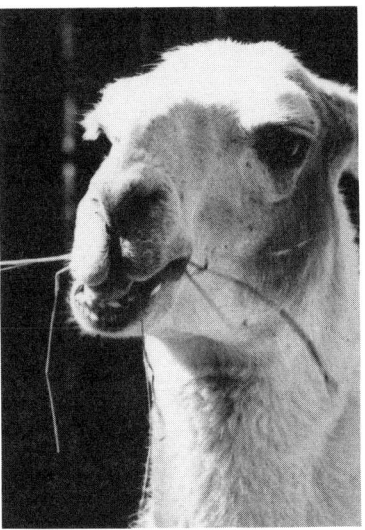

Meet Ned the Nerd

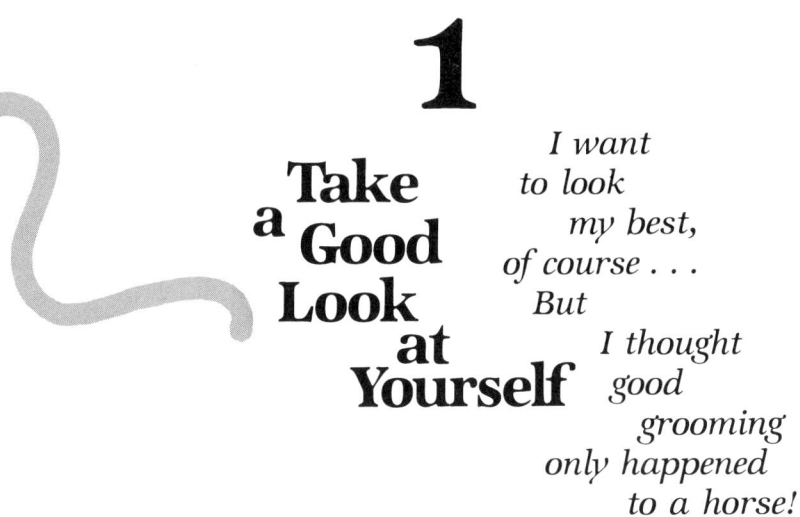

1
Take a Good Look at Yourself

I want to look my best, of course... But I thought good grooming only happened to a horse!

Gordon "Grubbles" Murphy walked into Mrs. Peoples' first-period English class and plopped down into his seat. His friend, Ian, leaned across the aisle and whispered, "Hey, Grub! You really look trashed today."

Melissa "Foxy" Rogers giggled. "Grubbles always looks trashed," she said. Her voice carried across the room.

Mrs. Peoples was writing an assignment on the board. The homework for the weekend was to write a composition entitled, "Why Good Grooming Is Important to Me." Mrs. Peoples gave Gordon a long look. "I expect **everybody** to turn in this assignment on Monday. No excuses!"

Gordon sighed. "What a lousy way to blow a weekend," he complained after class.

Melissa laughed. "It shouldn't take **you** long, Grubbles. Good grooming obviously isn't important to you at all."

Gordon put the assignment out of his mind until Sunday afternoon. He was sitting at the kitchen table with a blank piece of paper in front of him when his little sister, Dodie, walked in.

"I hope you won't be in here long," she said, wrinkling up

her nose. "Mom hates to fumigate." She looked curiously over his shoulder. "Whatcha doin', Grub?"

Gordon groaned. "I have to write a dumb composition on why good grooming is important to me."

Dodie laughed so hard she held her sides. "That's really easy. You can do it in three words: IT DOESN'T MATTER!"

"Cut that out, Dodie! This is serious stuff. I don't want to flunk English . . . again."

Dodie stopped laughing. "OK, big brother, if you really want some help, you came to the right person. Let's face it— you've let yourself go. You've got a bad case of the grubbies, but we may have caught it in time."

She stepped closer and stared at him. "I think there's hope," she finally said. "I wouldn't say this in public, but you're really not bad looking. All you have to do is get your act together." Suddenly she looked inspired. "Hey, Gordie,

Taking a Good Look at Yourself

you can write a case history and call it 'The Transformation of Grubbles Murphy.'"

Gordon didn't laugh.

"OK, OK," Dodie said. "No more jokes. Let's get down to business." She put her hands on her hips. "For starters, let's check your toes. I'll bet they're stuck together, and I **know** you need a bath."

She came closer and sniffed. "While you're at it, get wet all over and use some soap!

"Don't forget to

wash your hair,
clean your nails,
brush your teeth,
shave the fuzz off your chin,
put on clean clothes—

and, Gordie, has Dad ever had a talk with you about deodorant?"

"Aw, Dodie. I know all that stuff."

Dodie can be a real pain, Gordon thought, *but sometimes the kid comes up with a good idea or two. A case history might not be such a bad idea.* Walking into the bathroom, he slammed the door shut and locked it. Then he began to run hot water in the tub. *Might as well go all the way,* he thought. *What do I have to lose?*

At first, Gordon expected the hot water to irritate his skin and the shampoo to burn his eyes and blind him for life. He didn't intend to use the scrub brush at all, and he was afraid he would cut his throat shaving.

To his surprise, the water felt good, the shampoo was tearproof, the scrub brush had soft bristles, and he shaved his chin like a pro.

When he put on clean clothes and gave himself a quick once-over in front of the hall mirror, Gordon was surprised by what he saw. He was also surprised by the way he felt.

"Hmmm," Gordon murmured. "Not bad. Not bad at all."

That night, when Gordon was working on his composition, his dad walked by twice just to look him over. "Way to go, Gordie," he said.

When Dodie looked over Gordon's shoulder to see what he was writing, she saw: "The Transformation of Grubbles Murphy—a Case History."

"All righ-h-ht!" she exclaimed.

The next day Mrs. Peoples said Gordon's composition was the most interesting she had read in a long time. "My, my," she said, "you had a lot to write about, I guess."

When Melissa "Foxy" Rogers saw him she stared hard, then gasped, "Gru . . . Gr . . . Gordon? Is that really you?" A book slipped out of her hand, and she waited while he scooped it up. "Tha-a-ank you, Gordie." She looked up at him and smiled.

"No problem, Meli. Any time you want to drop a book, I'll pick it up for you."

Melissa batted her eyes. "Are you going my way?"

"You bet I am!" Gordon replied.

Good grooming became important to Gordon because

he LOOKED better,
he FELT better,
and
he ACTED better.

What does good grooming mean to you?

Everyone has a grubby day now and then. But if you find yourself trashed out most of the time, like Grubbles Murphy, you may need a little remodeling.

Rate yourself on the Personal Pollution Rating Chart below and see if you need a minor tune-up or a major overhaul.

PERSONAL POLLUTION RATING CHART

Instructions: Select the answers that best describe your good or not-so-good habits. Enter the appropriate scores in the blanks at the right.

PART I: THE BODY BEAUTIFUL

1. Showering or bathing (with soap)
   - daily .... 5 _____
   - several times a week .... 3 _____
   - weekly .... 1 _____
   - splashing, sponging, or hosing .... 0 _____

2. Shampooing hair
   - four or more times a week .... 5 _____
   - three times a week .... 3 _____
   - once a week .... 1 _____
   - only when caught in the rain .... 0 _____

3. Brushing teeth (with toothpaste)
   - after every meal .... 5 _____
   - morning and night .... 3 _____
   - once a day .... 1 _____
   - before going to the dentist .... -2 _____

4. Using deodorant
   - daily .... 5 _____
   - several times a week .... 3 _____
   - weekly .... 1 _____
   - drowning in cologne instead .... -1 _____

5. Changing underwear and socks
   daily .... 5 ____
   weekly .... 1 ____
   on national holidays .... 0 ____
   when stiff .... -5 ____

6. Caring for fingers and toes
   daily maintenance .... 5 ____
   clean and cut before Grandma visits .... 0 ____
   biting or tearing .... -5 ____

PART II: THE OUTER WRAPPINGS

1. Mending tears and pulled seams
   as soon as possible .... 5 ____
   after the next wash .... 2 ____
   only if embarrassing .... 1 ____
   pinning or supergluing .... -3 ____

2. Sewing on buttons
   when still loose .... 5 ____
   soon after they fall off .... 3 ____
   when you don't have anything
      else to wear .... 1 ____
   throwing garment in dirty
      clothes hamper .... -2 ____

3. Cleaning clothes
   daily spot inspection .... 5 ____
   ring around the collar .... 0 ____
   your clothes can stand alone .... -5 ____

4. Storing clothes
   neatly folded in closet or drawers .... 5 ____
   draped over chair .... 1 ____
   tossed on floor .... 0 ____
   stuffed under bed, in closet,
      or other secret place .... -5 ____

Taking a Good Look at Yourself

Now add up all your points and divide your total score by 10. If you got 4.5 or more, consider yourself well groomed. If you got 4.2 to 4.4, there are a few flaws in your system, but a quick tune-up should make things right. If your score was 4.1 or less, you need to rethink the way you feel about yourself. Read over the chart and find ways to improve your daily grooming habits.

Spend a little time on *you*. You're worth it!

Clean up your appearance,
　Then clean up your act;
Good grooming is easy—
　Now that is a fact.
You'll never be sorry
　You spent time on you,
When you look better, feel better,
　And act better, too.

2
Let's Shake on It

*I look upon
every day
to be lost
in which
I do not make
a new
acquaintance.*

—Samuel Johnson

All living creatures have ways of saying "hello . . . pleased to meet you . . . how do you do . . . nice to see you again. . . ." These greetings are called **salutations.**

When your dog sees you, it probably wags its tail and gives you a big lick. Your cat might rub against your legs and purr a lot. People often kiss, pat, or hug each other when they are good friends. Bears and pythons are also known for their hugs, but a hug from one of those might ruin your day.

The llama and the camel have strange ways of greeting people. If they don't like your looks, they will spit in your eye. But for the pastoral Masai people of East Central Africa, spitting is a friendly way to say "hello" or "good-bye."

In India, people greet each other by putting the palms of their hands together, fingers upward, and bowing their heads. The traditional greeting in Japan is a bow from the waist. In ancient China, people touched their foreheads to the ground to show their respect. This was called kowtowing. In

the Middle East, the salaam is a ceremonial greeting made by placing the right hand on the forehead and bowing low. In days gone by, rubbing noses was an affectionate greeting among Eskimos, Mongols, and many Indo-Chinese.

Pilots dip their plane's wings to greet each other, and soldiers salute. Saluting goes back to medieval days when knights in armor put their hands to their foreheads and raised their visors in greeting. When men tip their hats today, they are following the same custom.

In the animal kingdom, the sow bug has only one greeting, and that's "good-bye!"

It doesn't like intros at all;
It rolls itself into a ball . . .
Tucks in its feet and
  tucks in its head.
If you didn't know better,
  You'd think it was dead.

The sow bug says "good-bye" before it has a chance to get acquainted. A disappearing act like that is not a great way to make friends.

Fortunately, most people are not like sow bugs.

They like to have friends.
They like to make new friends.
They like to see their friendship
  trees grow!

On the next two pages is a typical friendship tree. You might want to use this pattern to make one of your own. Simply add as many leaves as you need to the branches and insert the names of your friends on the leaves. Include old friends as well as new ones. And remember—relatives are friends, too!

Growing your friendship tree can be difficult if you don't know how to meet people. Introductions are often at the root of the problem.

Over the years people have made rules for greeting each other. These rules have grown and grown until now people GROAN when they try to remember them.

Let's Shake on It

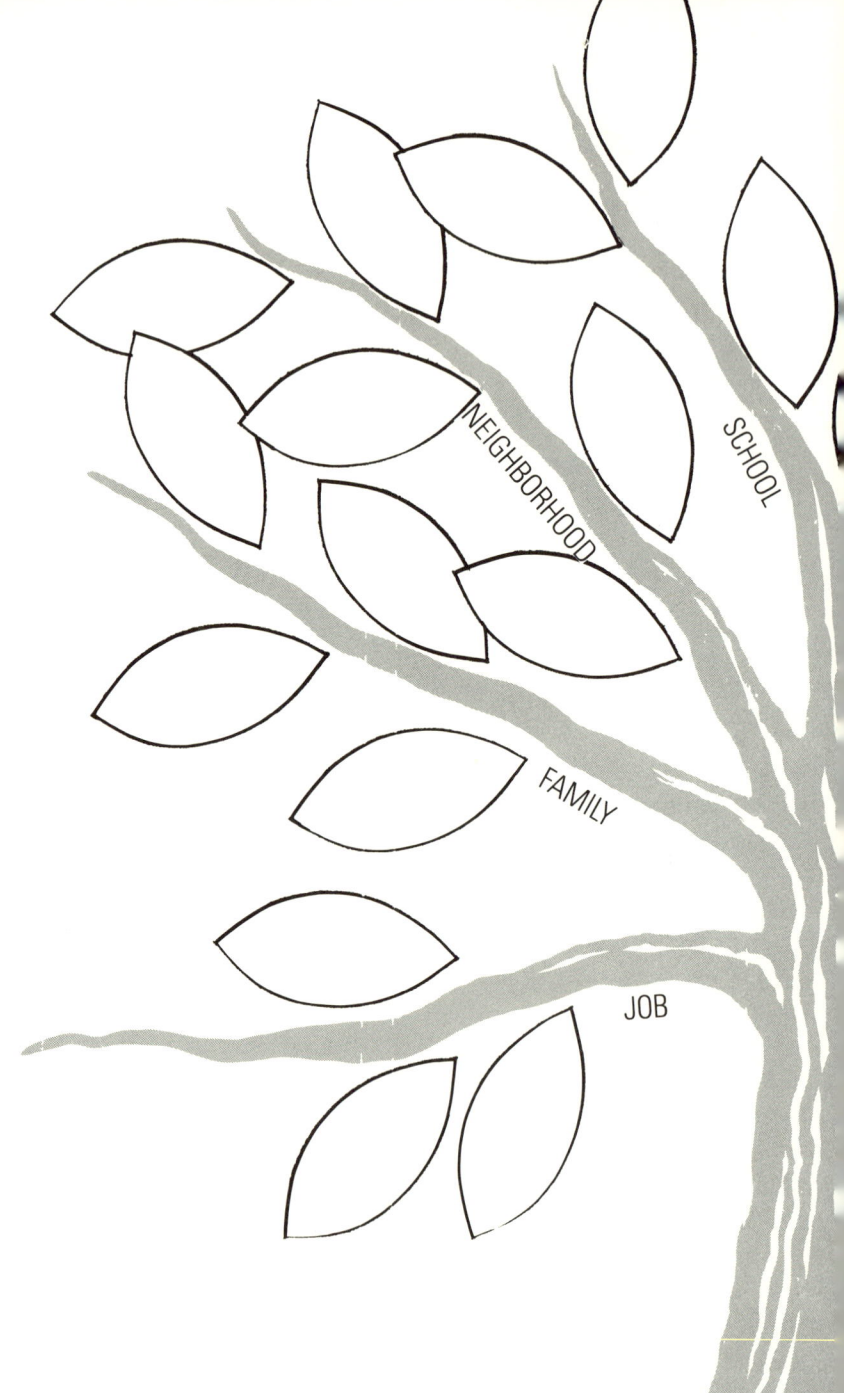

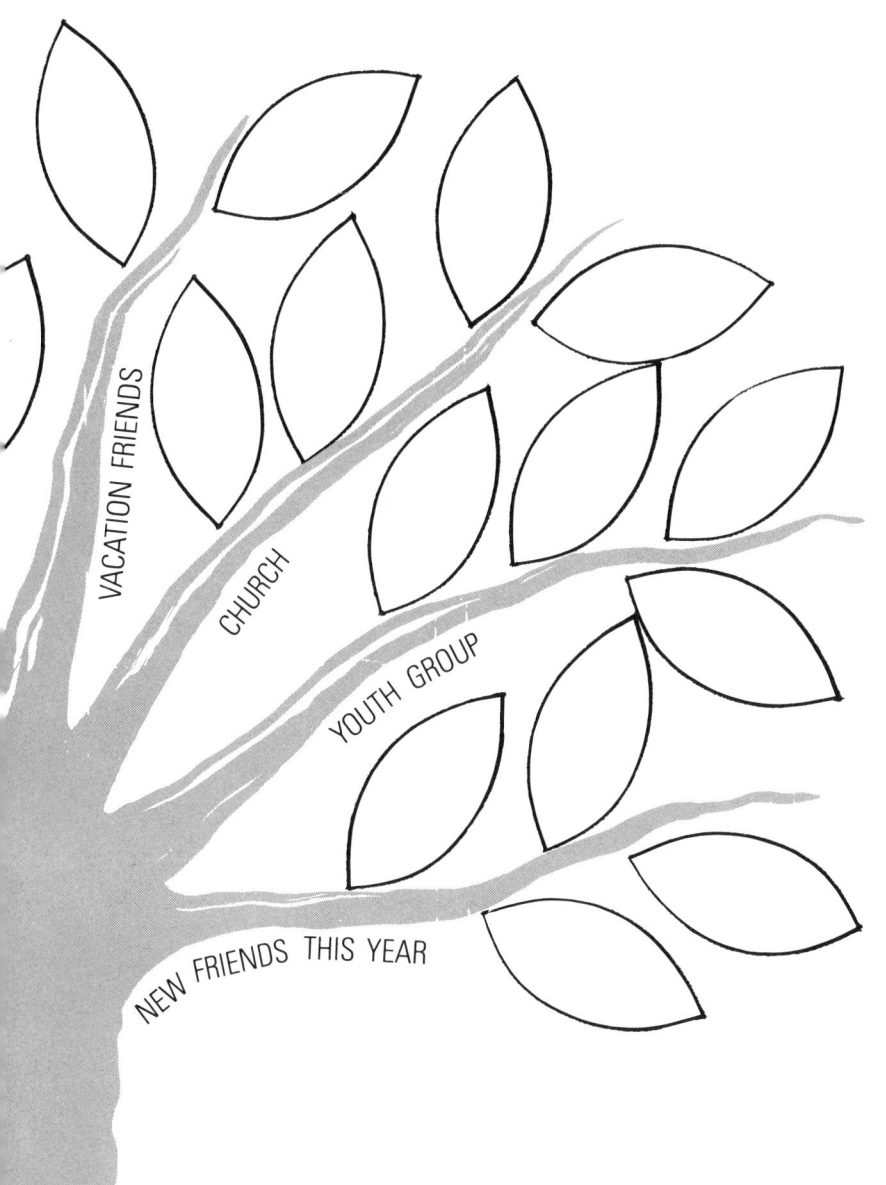

The truth is, many of the old rules don't work anymore. Take this one, for example:

When you pass a lady, always tip your hat with your right hand because your left hand will be holding the reins of your horse.

The rules that work today seem to have one thing in common. They help people feel comfortable when they meet each other. Here are a few easily managed rules that will make introductions easier for you.

Making Introductions

1. Say a woman's (or girl's) name before a man's (or boy's). "Dina Jones, I'd like you to meet Conrad Smith."
2. Say an older person's name before a younger person's name. "Dad, I'd like you to meet Dina Jones and Conrad Smith."
3. Say a newcomer's name before the names of others in your group of friends. "Lucy, I want you to meet Madge, Dina, Bill, and Conrad."
4. When the group is a large one, it is perfectly OK to say: "Hey, guys, this is Conrad Smith!" or, "Listen, everybody! I want you to meet Dina Jones and Conrad Smith."
5. If a person has a title, you should use it. "Colonel Pierce, I'd like you to meet my friend, Lucy," or, "Grandmother, I want you to meet Dr. Jones."
6. If you forget someone's name, the world won't come to an end. Just smile and say, "I'm really sorry. I can't remember your name," or, "I really know your name—I just can't seem to think of it!"
7. When you say a person's name, speak up so people can hear it.
8. When the introductions are over, it's up to you to get the conversation started. You can do this by telling the people something about each other, such as: "Dina's new in town. Her family just moved into the old Linden House," or, "Conrad plays a mean game of tennis. You two should get together for a few sets sometime," or, "Bill just came in from Japan. His dad's in the service, too."

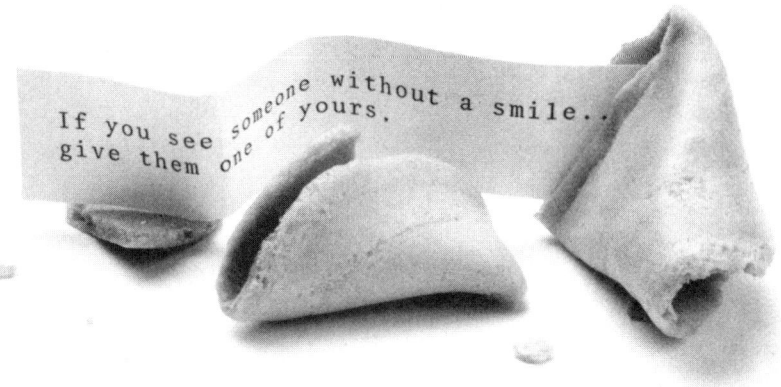

Being Introduced
1. **Boys should always stand up** when being introduced.
2. **Girls should always stand up** when being introduced to an older person.
3. **Men and boys shake hands** with each other.
4. **Women and girls offer their hands** if they want to shake.
5. **As soon as you are introduced,** you should say something pleasant, such as

   "How do you do?"
   "Nice to meet you."
   "Hello."
   or just plain "Hi!"

6. **If you are introduced to someone really important,** you don't have to grovel, salaam, or kowtow. But you might want to say something appropriate, such as: "It's an honor to meet you, Mr. President."
7. **If the person introducing you forgets your name,** volunteer it quickly. This will save both of you from embarrassment.
8. **If you don't hear the other person's name,** don't play guessing games. Simply say, "I'm sorry. I didn't hear your name."
9. **When you end a conversation with a new acquaintance,** remember to say something like, "Nice to have met you," or, "See you again soon!"
10. **Above all, SMILE!** Nobody likes to meet someone with a sour face.

Self-introductions
When no one is around to introduce you and you see someone you want to meet, you can:

Find a friend to do the honors.
Introduce yourself.

Introductions are simple ways of getting to know new people. They help your friendship tree grow. The more you practice, the easier introductions will be.

Let's Shake on It

She before he . . . you before me,
Remember their names, or sorry you'll be.
"Miss Smith, Mr. Jones, I'd like you to meet . . ."
There are so many ways to learn how to greet.

Tip your hat, take a bow,
Say, "How do you do?"
"My pleasure, I'm sure,"
or "It's nice meeting you."
If you make a mistake and get real uptight,
There are dozens of ways of making things right.
Just try to remember: be friendly and kind.
Whatever your mishap, no one will mind.

3

Chitchat

When introductions are over, what happens next?
CONVERSATION enables people to

share experiences,
share information,
share common interests,
share likes and dislikes,
  and
become friends.

Unfortunately, conversation is not always as easy as it sounds. Billy puts his hands in his pockets and stares at his feet. Miriam giggles a lot. Andrea is a motormouth—she talks all the time but says nothing. And then there's Sid, who can only talk about the weather. Picture these four kids together, each one doing his or her thing.

Are **you** ever at a loss for the right words? When you have to talk to someone you don't know very well, do you freeze up, giggle, or say all the wrong things?

Cheer up! This chapter is going to show you how to

start a conversation,
keep it going,
be a good listener,
  and
avoid gossip!

How to Start a Conversation
It takes two or more people to have a conversation, but only one clever person to get things rolling. A good conversation starter knows the difference between a

Dead-End Question
  and an
Open-Ended Question.

A **dead-end question** is like a dead-end street. The conversation goes to the end of the road and comes to a screeching stop. Here are some examples of the way dead-end questions sound.

Question: "What's your favorite TV show?"
Answer: "My Favorite Spy." (dead-end)

Question: "Nice party, huh?"
Answer: "Yep." (dead-end)

Question: "Do you like to play tennis?"
Answer: "Nope." (dead-end)

How can you know if you are asking a dead-end question? That's easy. A dead-end question can be answered in one or two words. It doesn't take the conversation anywhere.

An **open-ended question** is like a highway. It makes room for

answers,
explanations,
opinions,
and
ideas

to travel freely in both directions.
Here are some examples of open-ended questions:

"**Can you tell me,** Bill, about the time you spent in Japan?"
"**Can you tell me** about the old Linden House, Dina? I've never been inside."
"**What do you think** Mrs. Thiggleby's going to quiz us on tomorrow?"
"**What do you think** we should have to eat at the party?"
"**Which classes** are you taking this semester?"
"**Why do you think** the Celtics have won so many championships?"
"**How do you find** time to practice four hours every day?"

Open-ended questions open the door to conversations. They get you going and take you somewhere. They let other people know you are interested in them.

Conversation Starting Tips
Do remember the other person's name and use it occasionally.
Do ask about the other person's interests or hobbies.

The Right Way to Eat Spaghetti

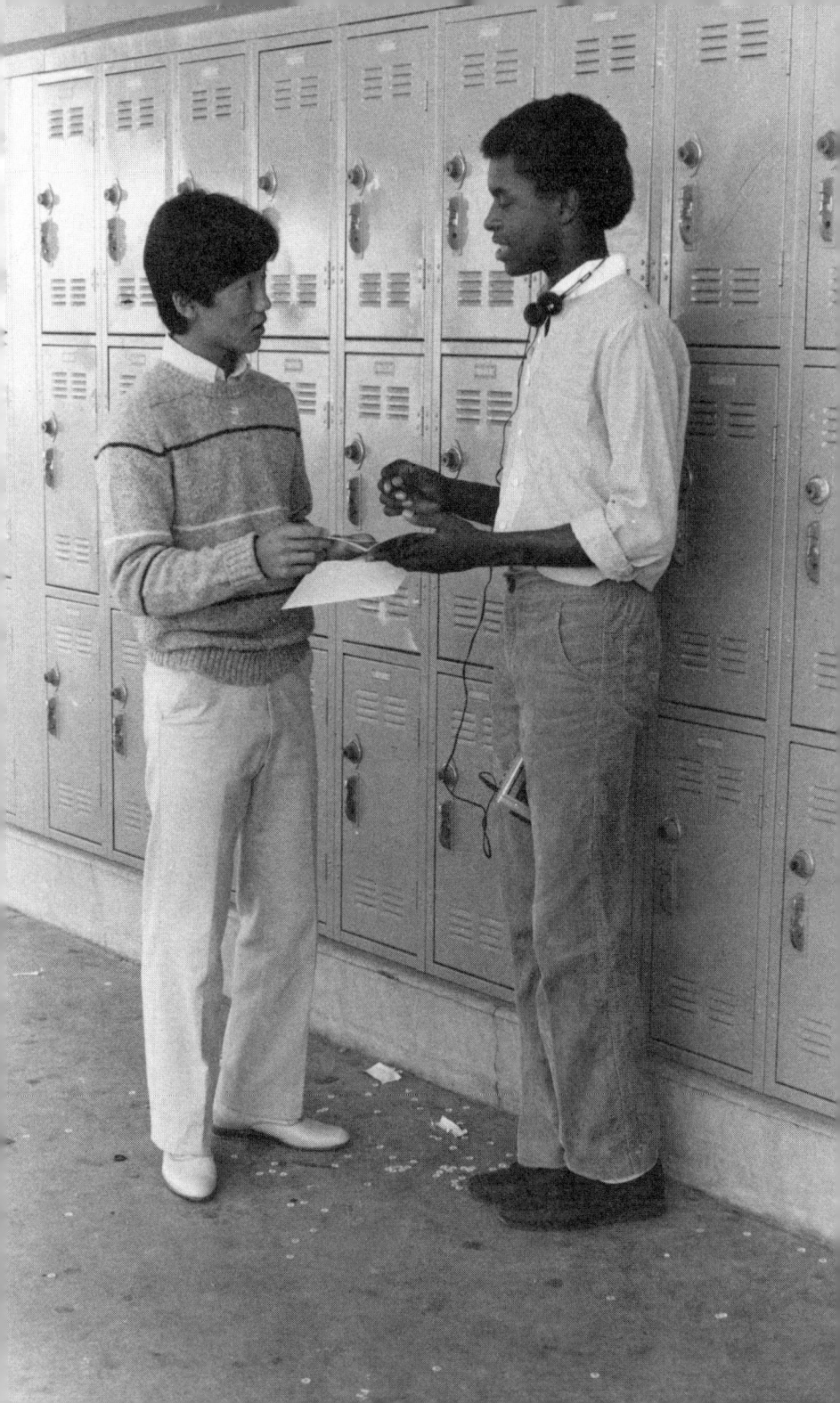

Do introduce subjects you have in common (teachers, classes, books, sports, movies, or music).
Don't look at your shoes or the ceiling when you meet a new acquaintance.

How to Keep Conversation Going
Sometimes conversations start out with a bang, then quickly run out of steam. You can avoid this problem if you learn the art of **chaining.**

Chaining is the process by which a conversation is renewed when it begins to die. Here is a diagram of a conversation that didn't have a chance to develop. It looks like a single link that became separated from its chain.

A. Start
B. Enthusiasm rising
C. Peak
D. Enthusiasm declining
E. Awkward silence

Whenever a conversation seems to be going downhill (D) and you feel an awkward silence approaching, you can keep enthusiasm up by injecting BOOSTER SHOTS of

new information,
a funny story,
an expert opinion,
or
a question.

Some good conversation boosters:

"That reminds me of the joke about..."
"I read in the newspaper that..."
"According to Dr. Reinhold..."
"Where did you learn so much about...?"

Booster shots keep your conversation going forward and upward, instead of downhill into an awkward silence. When you add booster shots to your conversation, it looks like a whole chain with all the links connected:

See if you can think of some booster shot ideas that might work for you.

BOOSTER SHOT IDEAS TO REMEMBER
1. _____
2. _____
3. _____
4. _____
5. _____

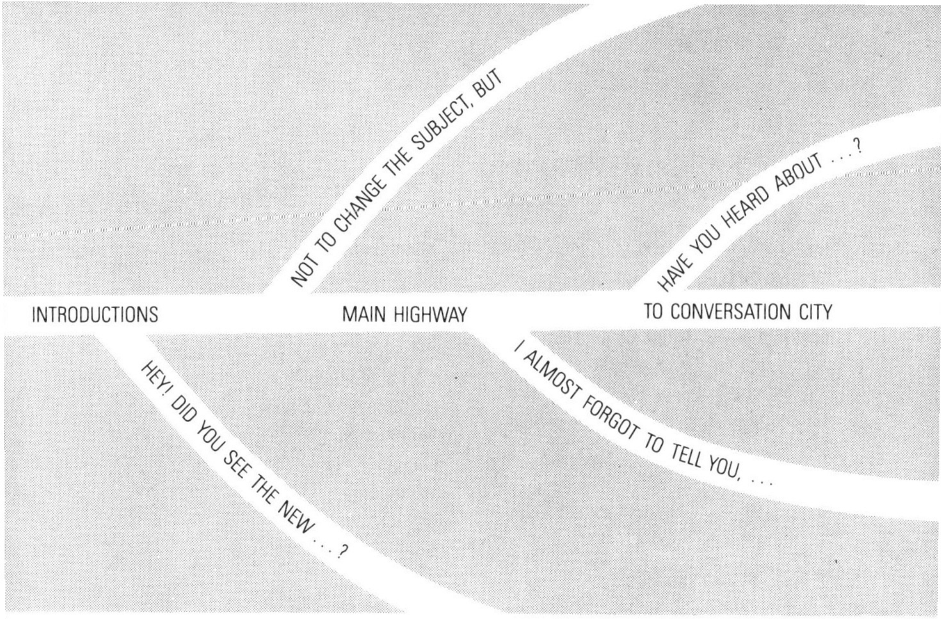

INTRODUCTIONS — NOT TO CHANGE THE SUBJECT, BUT ... — MAIN HIGHWAY — HAVE YOU HEARD ABOUT ... ? — TO CONVERSATION CITY

HEY! DID YOU SEE THE NEW ... ?

I ALMOST FORGOT TO TELL YOU, ...

A Cure for Boredom
Sometimes a subject becomes boring, and even the best-aimed booster shot misses its mark. When this happens, you need to reach into your bag of tricks and use the technique called **branching out**.

Alternate routes provide new, exciting ways of seeing the countryside. Branching out is like taking an alternate route or new direction to Conversation City.

Study the road map and see if you can think of some alternate routes of your own, ways to change the subject in a conversation.

Write **your** alternate routes in the spaces provided:

1. _____

2. _____

3. _____

4. _____

5. _____

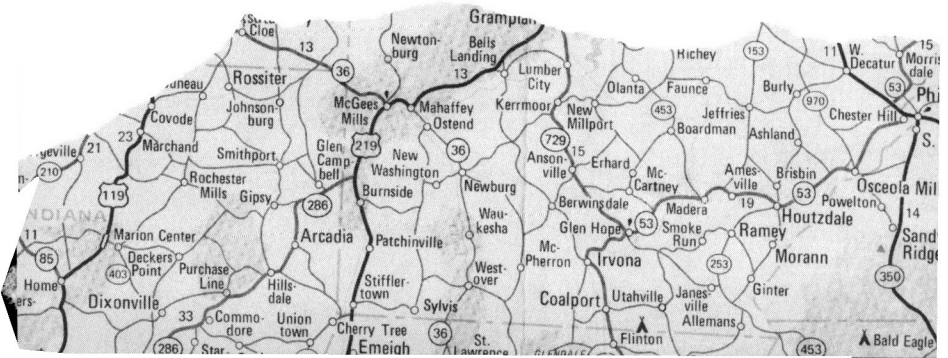

Talking Tips
Do admit it if you don't hear what is being said:

"I'm sorry; I couldn't hear you,"
"I beg your pardon," or
"Excuse me."

Do speak up so people can hear you.
Do say, "thank you" when you receive a compliment.
Do have the courage to state your opinions and feelings. Join the conversation!
Do avoid profanity. Crude words have no place in good conversation.
Do remember to smile.
Don't chew gum while you're talking. If you have gum in your mouth, don't pop it, and don't let it show.
Don't say, "what?" "huh?" "whazzat?"
Don't talk about a private subject in front of people who aren't involved. They will feel left out.
Don't ask personal questions that are none of your business, such as: "How much money does your dad make?" or, "How much do you weigh?"
Don't brag or exaggerate. Tell it like it is.

How to Be a Good Listener
A conversation requires two things: a speaker and a listener.
  When it's your turn to be a listener, be a good one. Here are seven simple **Hearing Aids** that will make people want to talk to you.
1. **Do** look at the person who is speaking. This means **don't** keep looking at your watch or glancing sideways.
2. **Don't** interrupt when someone else is speaking—unless there is a real emergency. If you must interrupt, say, "Excuse me."
3. **Do** listen to what the other person is saying. **Don't** think about the soccer game, the party Saturday night, the fly circling the punch bowl, or what Mary Lou Jones is wearing today.
4. **Do** respect the speaker's right to have an opinion—even if you don't agree. It's polite to say, "That's an interesting idea, Joe." It's not polite to say, "You've flipped your lid!"
5. **Don't** indulge in **one-upmanship.** One-upmanship means deliberately trying to top whatever someone says with a story that is better. One-upmanship is a sneaky way of putting another person down.
6. **Don't** turn on the TV, radio, or stereo unless **everyone** wants to listen.
7. **Don't** do anything that is distracting, such as

  popping your knuckles or joints,
  cleaning your fingernails or toenails,
  scratching any part of your body,
  picking at your teeth or nose,
  burping loudly,
  yawning, or
  clearing your throat over and over.

Distracting sounds and movements can be conversation killers.
  Everyone likes a good listener. Practice your hearing aids and you can become an expert.

How to Avoid Gossip
Gossip is bad manners of the worst kind. People who gossip like to talk about other people instead of ideas, events, opinions, hopes, plans, places, or things.

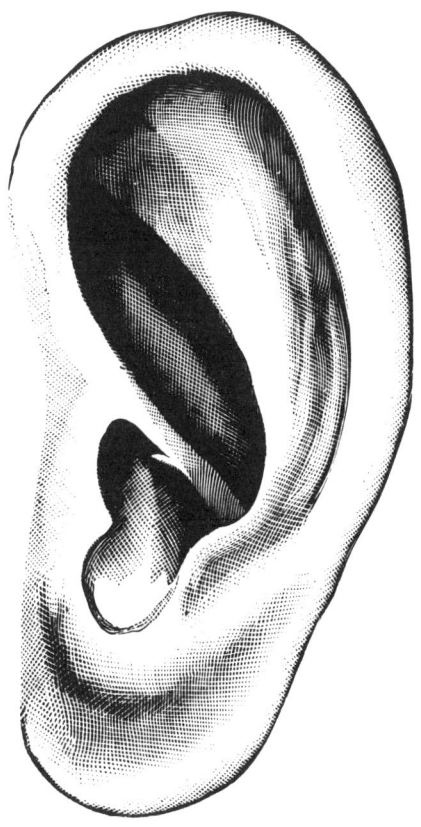

Chitchat

A gossip is called by many names. You have probably heard some of these:

TATTLETALE,
MEDDLER,
BUSYBODY,
SNOOP, and
TALEBEARER.

Gossips have even been given labels like:

STICKY-BEAK,
LONG-NOSE,
BLATHERSKITE,
PAUL PRY,
NEWSMONGER,
CONFABULATOR, and
TITTLE-TATTLE.

All of these titles describe the same kind of person—someone who spreads news that might injure someone else. You can see why a gossip has few friends. People soon learn that a gossip can't be trusted.

How Can You Avoid Being a Gossip?
1. **Stick to the facts.**
   Fact: "Mary is moving on Tuesday."
   Gossip: "I wonder why Mary has to leave town by Tuesday."
2. **Spread the good news.**
   Good news: "Sam won a free trip to Disneyland."
   Gossip: "I wonder what Sam had to do to get a free pass to Disneyland."
3. **Don't exaggerate.**
   Tell it like it is: "Bill makes three dollars when he mows the lawn for his dad."
   Gossip: "Bill's dad gives him piles of money."

HOW CAN YOU STOP GOSSIP ONCE IT HAS STARTED?
It's easy. All you have to say is, "Let's change the subject."

Changing the subject is the most polite way to stop the gossip grapevine from growing.

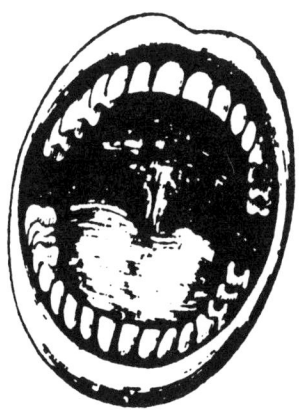

4
Tools of the Trade

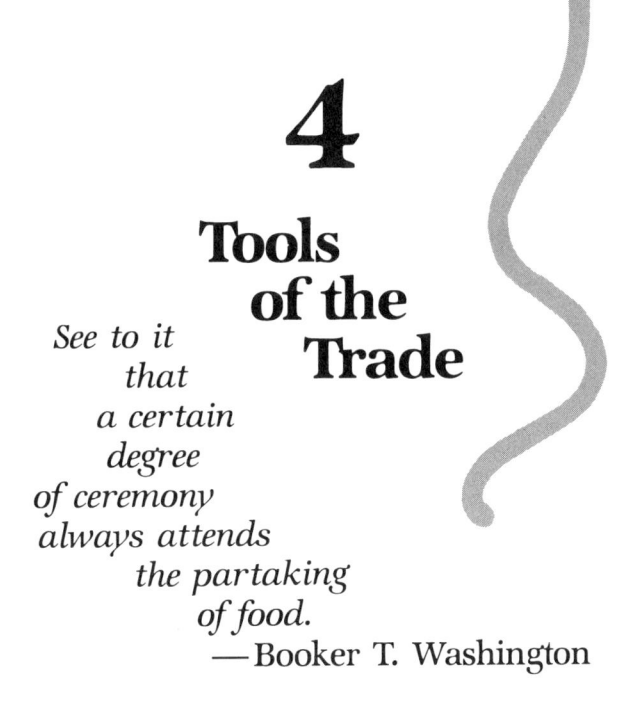

See to it that a certain degree of ceremony always attends the partaking of food.
—Booker T. Washington

People came equipped with eating tools. Early people probably used their fingers to put food into their mouths. Then someone discovered that drippy, gooey things could be handled more easily in leaves, shells, or gourds. This tidied up the table a little, but not much.

A good deal of tugging and gnawing still went on at mealtime until someone discovered that crude cutting tools could be made from sharp shells, bones, or stones.

The first forks were probably made of wood or bone and were used for spearing fish and cooking meat over the fire.

As centuries passed, the way many people ate became more complicated. The Greeks and Romans hammered spoons with pointed handles out of silver and gold.

During the Middle Ages in Europe, poor people had to make do with iron kitchen knives, but rich people had special little eating knives they carried around in sheaths. A small Scottish knife called a *sgian dubh* was used at mealtimes.

In those days, it was common practice at the table to hack off a piece of meat and throw it to your favorite dog.

After a while, there were so many special eating knives that people hardly knew what to do with them. There were

*fish knives,
meat knives,
fruit knives,
butter knives,
cheese knives,
dessert knives,
—and many more.*

Forks were used in Venice in the eleventh century, but when they first were introduced in England five hundred years later people laughed at them and thought they were silly.

In many parts of the Orient, people never use forks. Instead, they like to eat with chopsticks.

For a long time, Europeans couldn't put their food on plates because they didn't have any. Instead, they placed thick slices of bread called **tranchoirs** on the table and put the food on these. No need for a dishwasher! Much later, people used wooden platters called **trenchers.** At dessert time, they simply turned the trenchers upside down.

It wasn't until the Pilgrims came to America that knives, forks, and spoons appeared on the table at the same time. People became more and more conscious of their manners and the need for rules of behavior at the table.

Table Settings
Everyone should know how to properly set the table for a simple meal.

All the items should be arranged neatly on a tablecloth or placemat. The knife is always placed with the cutting edge facing the plate.

BASIC TABLE SETTING

There will be times when you will need to be familiar with a more formal American-type table setting.

1. napkin
2. fork
3. plate
4. knife
5. spoon
6. glass

FORMAL TABLE SETTING

1. napkin
2. salad fork
3. dinner fork
4. dinner plate
5. knife
6. teaspoon
7. soup spoon
8. salad plate
9. bread and butter plate (with knife)
10. glass

When you are faced with a complicated table setting, follow this basic rule for selecting knives, forks, and spoons: begin at the outside and work your way in.

Tools of the Trade 39

SLOPPY EATERS MAKE OTHER PEOPLE LOSE THEIR APPETITES!

Table Manners

Years ago, people in Japan were executed if they didn't have good table manners. Fortunately, this doesn't happen today. Good table manners are still important, however, and for good reason.

Don't be a sloppy eater. You can learn a few general **gastronomic guidelines*** that will make mealtimes more pleasant for you... and everyone around you, too. Let's start at the beginning.

*****Gastronomic** (gas-struh-NAH-mick) refers to the art of good eating.

Before the Fact

Jake didn't have any gastronomic guidelines at all. He raced into the house and slammed the door behind him, late for dinner again.

"Sorry about that," he mumbled as he slid into his chair. Suddenly he was aware that everyone was looking at him.

"Jake, you smell funny!" His little sister, Cindy, sniffed once, then put both hands over her nose.

The Right Way to Eat Spaghetti

"What's that black stuff all over your hands?" demanded Aunt Harriet.

"Young man, you're excused from this table until you get yourself cleaned up," his father ordered. "Wash your face and hands, comb your hair, and change that shirt!"

"Oh, Jake," his mother sighed.

Before you even think about coming to the table, you need to do three basic things:

1. **Wash** your hands (and face, if necessary).
2. **Comb** your hair.
3. **Check** your clothes to see if they will pass inspection.

Dinner Is Served

Even though you may be starved, there are a few preliminary rules you should be aware of. You're breaking the rules when you plop down in your chair and reach for the mashed potatoes before anyone else is even seated.

SEATING ARRANGEMENTS

1. It is good manners to wait until everyone is ready to sit down together.
2. If you are at a party, the hostess will tell you where to sit.

Tools of the Trade

3. Boys should seat girls—even at home. Here's how:

   *First, pull out the chair, then push it gently but firmly under the person when she starts to sit down. If she needs to sit closer, give the chair one more **small** push.*

4. Sit up straight. Put your feet on the floor. Try not to kick anybody.
5. Put your napkin on your lap. (If you're at a party, wait until the person at the head of the table picks up his or hers.) If it's a big napkin, unfold it only half way. A napkin should never be visible above your waist **unless** a special bib is provided for messy foods like:

   *lobster,
   barbequed ribs,
   corn on the cob, and
   fried chicken.*

6. Don't eat yet! If a prayer is to be offered before the meal, this is the usual time.
7. Don't take your first bite until the host or hostess starts eating or tells everyone to begin.

SHARING THE BOUNTY

Even passing the food has some simple rules to ensure that everyone will get a portion—with the least possible mess.

1. When it's your turn to serve yourself from a serving dish, **do** take the portion closest to you. **Don't reach** across the plate, even if the choicest morsels are on the far side. **Do** leave plenty for others.
2. If both a fork and spoon are on the serving dish,

   - **use the spoon** to scoop up your portion.
   - **use the fork** as a helping hand.
   - **replace them carefully** so that they won't do a swan dive while the plate is in midair.

3. Pass the serving dish to the person on your right.
4. A boarding house reach is a no-no. If you can't reach something easily, ask for it politely by saying, "May I have some vegetables, please?" or, "Will you please pass the salt?"

**REMEMBER—
Don't let your derriere ever leave the chair!**

The Ins and Outs

... OF SOUP:

The trick with soup is getting it from the bowl to the mouth without an *oops!*

1. Don't hold the spoon in your fist. Hold it like a pencil. Put it between your first and second fingers, and balance it with your thumb.
2. Dip from the bowl in the direction away from you.
3. Eat from the side of the spoon, not the tip, and all the while...
4. Keep your elbow close to your body, not in your neighbor's ribs. If a clear soup is served in a cup that has a handle, it is OK to pick it up and sip it ... but SILENTLY! Slurping is bad manners!

... OF MEAT AND FISH:

It is OK to cut two or three (no more!) pieces of meat at one time, lay your knife on the plate, then pick up your fork with the same hand and begin eating. This is American-style eating and is sometimes called the Big Switch.

It is also OK to cut your meat with your knife in one hand and put the fork in your mouth with the other hand. This is the European style.

Fish should be cut with a fork, one small piece at a time. If the fish has bones, it is OK to use your knife to remove them. At some dinners a special fish knife will be part of the table setting. It looks like this:

... OF SPAGHETTI:
Spaghetti is such a popular food that it deserves a special word—or two, or three.

Word 1: Dip and twist a reasonable amount around your fork, using a large spoon in the other hand as a backstop.

Word 2: Don't hold a forkful of spaghetti above your head and eat from the bottom up.

Word 3: Don't slurp.

... OF VEGETABLES:
You should eat most vegetables with your fork. Use your spoon only if a juicy vegetable like stewed tomatoes, rhubarb, or creamed corn is served in a side dish.

Salads are eaten with a fork, but you can use your knife if you need to cut up any large pieces.

Keep your vegetables in separate piles on your plate.

When vegetables such as asparagus, carrots, broccoli, or potatoes are served whole, cut them into bite-sized pieces. Never pick up the whole piece on your fork and eat it like a hot dog on a stick.

Never mix your vegetables with your mashed potatoes or pile food on the back of your fork or knife.

Some vegetables can be eaten with your fingers, which brings us to the ins and outs

... OF FINGER FOODS:
Raw vegetables are considered finger foods when they are served before dinner with a dip, or on a side dish at the table. Some **cooked vegetables** can also be eaten with your fingers. The most popular are

artichokes,
corn on the cob,
and
french fried potatoes.

Artichoke hearts should be eaten with your fork.

Tools of the Trade

When french fries are too big to handle, you should cut them and eat them with a fork.

Meat is sometimes a finger food. You can use your fingers for meat like:

crisp fried chicken drumsticks
  (or other small pieces),
ribs (hold them corncob style),
fried shrimp (use the tail as a
  handle),
bacon (if it is crisp), and
lobster or crab claws (use a little
  fork to get at the meat).

Some of these foods are messy. Many restaurants will provide you with finger bowls (small bowls of water to rinse your fingers in). Dip your fingers carefully in the water, and dry them on your napkin. A finger bowl is not a wash basin. Sometimes you will even get a special bib to keep messy foods off your clothes.

Fruits that are cooked are always eaten with a spoon. Fresh fruits such as grapefruit and melons are also best eaten with a spoon. Most other fruits are finger foods, but even these may require special handling at the table.

Bananas can be sliced into a bowl, or peeled, and broken into two or three bite-sized pieces. Only at picnics and at sack lunch time should you start at one end and chew your way to the other.

Apples and pears should be sliced and cored with a knife at the table. Otherwise, bite right in!

Oranges and tangerines can be peeled with your fingers and eaten one segment at a time.

Grapes are eaten one by one. Never hold a cluster above your head and nibble from it.

Strawberries are only eaten with your fingers if they have stems for handles.

Apricots can be easily split and the large pits removed. Eat one half at a time.

Pomegranates should be taken outside and carefully enjoyed. Wear your old clothes.

Plums can be eaten a bite at a time.

Cherries can be eaten whole, one at a time.

Fast foods are generally finger foods. Here are some favorites:

*hamburgers,
hot dogs,
french fries,
fish and chips,
onion rings,
pizza,
chicken in a basket,
tacos,
and tostados.*

These foods are designed to be eaten with as little formality as possible. But when any of these are too big or too juicy to hold in your hands, they should be eaten with a fork.

When you order food to "take out," remember to clean up your debris. Littering is against the law . . . and bad manners, besides.

You can also use your fingers for bread, cookies, nuts, crackers, pickles, sandwiches, chips and dip, and toothpick tidbits.

Try to remember not to recycle your chips! Once you have dipped and tasted, that chip is all yours forever. Nobody wants to see it make another trip to the bowl after it has been in your mouth.

... OF INDIGESTIBLES

Indigestibles are disagreeable things like bones, pits, gristle, and unchewable meat. Everyone is faced with an indigestible from time to time. The trick is knowing how to get rid of it. Here are three easy rules for you to follow.

Tools of the Trade

1. Stones, pits, or seeds from fruit that is being eaten with a spoon should be removed with a spoon.
2. If you are eating finger fruit, remove the pits or seeds with your fingers.
3. Anything else you can't swallow should be removed (with fingers or spoon) as quickly and inconspicuously as possible and put on your plate (under a lettuce leaf will do just fine).

What Do You Do When There's a Fly in Your Stew?
Don't broadcast your troubles to the world!

*Be quiet!
Be subtle!
Be careful!*

Simply lift out the offending object, put it on your plate (under the rim of your bowl), and forget about it. Whether or not you finish eating your stew . . . is up to you!

Disasters for all Occasions
Spilling, dropping, and slopping happen to everyone sooner or later.

When you have a dinnertime disaster, there are three things to remember:

*If you spill it, mop it up:
If you drop it, pick it up:
If you slop it, wipe it up.*

Don't come unglued. If your disaster is a big one, someone will usually come to your rescue.
Do apologize. You don't have to say any more than "I'm sorry," "Please forgive me," or, "I'm so sorry that happned."
Do offer to help clean up the mess.
Do offer to have clothing cleaned if your spill gets on someone else.

After the Fact
When you have finished your meal, put your knife and fork side by side across the top of the plate.
Put your napkin on the table to the left of the plate.
Don't refold it.
  Don't wad it up into a ball.
    Don't leave it on the
      seat of your chair.
If you have to leave the table before dinner is over, say, "May I please be excused?"
Unless an emergency arises, you should wait until the host or hostess stands up before you leave the table. Remember to thank the host or hostess for your meal . . . regardless of how you felt about what you ate.

Leftovers

*If you close your mouth when it's full of food,
You'll put everyone in a better mood.
Don't use your bread to mop up your plate*

The Right Way to Eat Spaghetti

*Or "not invited" will soon be your fate.
No gnashing of teeth or slurping of soup—
Burping out loud is for nincompoops!*

*Sit up real straight, put your feet on the floor,
Tuck in your elbows, who could ask for more?
The food on your fork should be the right size;
Don't try to win the Biggest Bite Prize.
Cut with your knife and eat with your fork
Whether you're dining on beef, fowl, or pork.*

*Butter your bread one piece at a time—
Not the whole thing! You're doing just fine.
Don't sniff at your food before the first bite;
It's very bad manners—it's just not quite right.
Sit up in your chair; don't tip it way back,
Or you'll be on the floor, heaped in a stack.*

*A word about catsup is overdue;
It's everyone's favorite—that is true.
But when sauces and gravies are already served,
Forget the red stuff! Don't say that word!
And speaking of gravy—don't use too much;
You'll drown peas and carrots and spinach and such.*

*It's awfully easy to do the right stuff,
Just get in the habit—it isn't real tough.
Besides, when you're eating and in a good mood,
You're sure to enjoy more of your food.
So practice good manners, and one afternoon
You'll hear a friend say, "Please come again soon!"*

5

Let's Party!

Parties should be fun for everyone. They are times for
getting together with old friends,
celebrating special occasions,
making new friends,
sharing experiences,
telling stories,
looking at girls (or boys),
playing games,
eating,
listening,
laughing, and . . .
enjoying the company of other people.

Parties are more fun for everyone when people practice good party manners. These include

good hostmanship
as well as
good guestmanship.

It means thinking about other people and not doing foolish things that can ruin a perfectly good get-together.

Party Poopers come in all shapes and sizes. They can be party givers as well as party goers. You can avoid being a Party Pooper by following a few simple **Guidelines to Great Parties.**

GUIDELINES FOR PARTY GIVERS

HOW TO PLAN YOUR PARTY
Why are you having a party, anyway? Is it

someone's birthday,
back to school,
end of school,
maple sugar time,
Christmas,
Valentine's Day,
kite-flying season,
an important anniversary?

It's fun to choose a seasonal or holiday THEME and plan your party around it. The following PARTY WHEEL will give you some party theme suggestions. You may want to fill in the open spaces with ideas of your own.

Spin the wheel and pick a party!

There are many things you can do to make your party successful. Let's talk about...

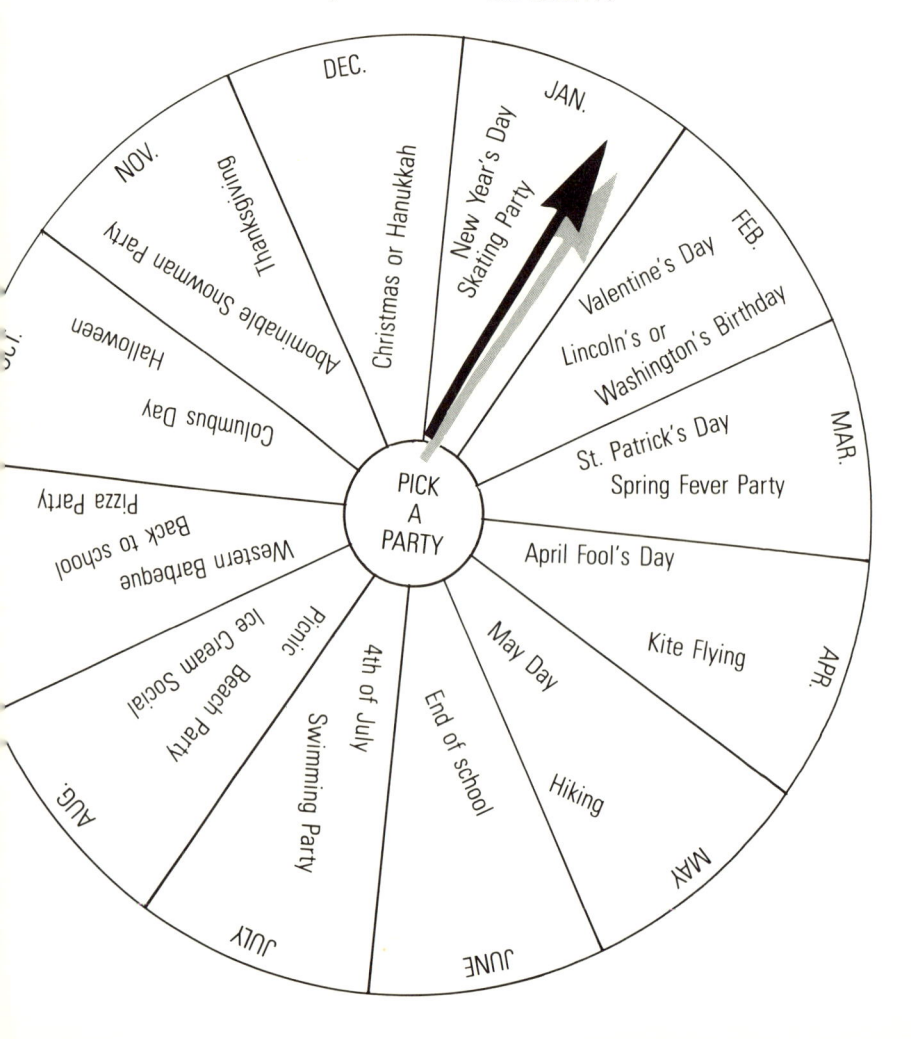

PICK A PARTY

- JAN. — New Year's Day Skating Party
- FEB. — Valentine's Day / Lincoln's or Washington's Birthday
- MAR. — St. Patrick's Day / Spring Fever Party
- APR. — April Fool's Day / Kite Flying
- MAY — May Day / Hiking
- JUNE — End of school
- JULY — 4th of July / Swimming Party
- AUG. — Picnic / Ice Cream Social / Beach Party
- (SEPT.) — Back to school / Pizza Party / Western Barbeque
- OCT. — Columbus Day / Halloween
- NOV. — Thanksgiving / Abominable Snowman Party
- DEC. — Christmas or Hanukkah

INVITATIONS

Last-minute parties can be fun, but they don't give you much time to plan, and some people won't be able to come on the spur of the moment. It's a good idea to give invitations by mail, phone, or in person at least one week ahead. No matter how you invite someone to your party, you should state

the date,
the time,
the place,
and
the reason for the party.

If your guests will need special clothes or a costume, be sure to tell them so.

RSVP is an abbreviation for *Répondez s'il vous plaît,* which means, Answer, if you please. It's a polite way of asking people to let you know whether or not they can come.

Be sure to send your invitations early. Don't make one of your guests feel like a second choice by waiting and inviting him or her at the last minute.

Let's Party!

YOU'RE INVITED TO A PARTY

Date *January 8*
Time *7:00 p.m. to 9:00 p.m.*
Place *Melissa Rogers' house*
112 Elmwood Drive
Belleville
Kind *Skating party (Bring your skates!)*
RSVP *555-4321*

DECORATIONS

Decorations are fun to make, especially when you ask your friends to help. Decorations don't need to be expensive. Colorful balloons, crepe paper streamers, hanging paper chains, and clever party favors all make a room look festive. You might want to create your own piñatas out of empty milk cartons. Here's how:

Wash and dry an empty carton.
Fill it with hard, wrapped candies.
Cover it with crepe paper twists, glued directly to the carton.
Use your imagination. Add button eyes, a paper hat, cardboard fins, or a rocket nose cone.
Fasten the piñata to one end of a rope. Toss the other end over a tree limb and let someone raise the piñata up and down while your blindfolded guests take turns trying to break it open with a stick. Scramble for the candies when they fall!

A piñata is a good decoration and also serves as an activity.

ACTIVITIES

Activities are only fun if everyone gets to join in. You should never have party games that only interest boys when girls are at the party, too. If the theme of your party **is** an activity (a skating party, for example), you probably won't have to worry about games. But here are a couple of quickies, just in case.

Memory Game
1. Place at least twenty small items on a tray.
2. Put the tray on a table and let everybody look at it for one minute.
3. Remove or cover the tray.
4. Pass out paper and pencils and ask your guests to write down as many items as they can remember.
5. Give a prize to the winner.

Variation of the Memory Game
Repeat steps 1, 2, and 3 from above.

4. Remove the tray and take away one item.
5. Return the tray to the table.
6. The winner is the first person to identify the missing item.

Copy Cat
1. Everyone sits in a circle.
2. The first player makes a motion (such as scratching his or her nose).
3. The second player scratches his nose, then adds a new motion (such as pulling his ear).
4. The third person repeats what the others have done, then adds another motion.
5. This continues around the room until someone "misses" and is "out."
6. The winner is the last person left.

Sometimes circumstances or the weather can sabotage your party. When this happens, it's time for Plan B; your alternate activity choice in case of an emergency.

PLAN B

—*If the rain spoils your picnic, can you move the party indoors?*
—*If the skating rink is closed, can you go to the river or beach?*
—*If the game you're playing is a dud, do you have another one up your sleeve?*

Plan B should never take advantage of your friends. Some of them may love to entertain at parties. All the same, it's not very thoughtful to expect them to help you out of every emergency. For example, if you want Joe to play the guitar for your guests, be sure to ask him ahead of time.

WHEN THE GUESTS ARRIVE

Be there,
Be ready,
and
Be welcoming.

1. Be there. A good host will always be there when the party starts. This is no time to remember something you need to do downtown.

2. Be ready. If your party is well planned, everything will be ready at least twenty minutes before it begins. This gives you time to mellow

Let's Party!   53

out before your first guest comes—or take care of any early arrivals. Don't forget to lock up any roaming pets that might become a nuisance.

3. Be welcoming. Answer the door yourself. Greet people with a smile. Invite them in. Make them glad they came. If your guests are carrying gifts or wearing coats, show them where to put those things. Making people welcome makes them feel at home.

AT THE PARTY

Remember to introduce people who don't know each other.

Try to see that no one feels left out.

Try to keep things moving. If your party bogs down, it's time for a change. Try serving food, playing a new game, changing the music.

Try to keep yourself moving. Don't talk to the same people all the time.

REMEMBER, this is **your** party! It's **your** responsibility to see that your guests have a good time.

GUIDELINES FOR PARTY GOERS

INVITATIONS

Start thinking about going to a party as soon as you receive the invitation. Now is the time to read it carefully . . . not the night before the party. Check the **date,** the **time,** the **place,** and whether or not a costume or **special clothing** is required. Check with your parents to make sure you have permission to go.

RSVP as soon as you can—even if the invitation doesn't ask you to.

If your answer is YES, be sure to: thank the person for inviting you; offer to help with decorations, food, games, entertainment, or even cleaning up after the party; and inquire about what type of clothing to wear, if you don't already know.

If your answer is NO, be sure to: thank the person for inviting you, say you are sorry you can't come, and give a reason if you have one.

WHEN YOU ARRIVE

Be on time,
Be dressed appropriately, and
Be prepared.

1. **Be on time.** A good guest tries to be on time. Late arrivals have to make an awkward entrance. Early arrivals are apt to be in the way. The best time to arrive is when your host asks you to.

2. **Be dressed appropriately.** Did you recheck your invitation to see if you are dressed appropriately? Old clothes are not right for dress-up parties, and costumes are out of place at most birthday parties. If your invitation doesn't spell it out, don't be afraid to ask what the other guests will be wearing.

3. **Be prepared.** Before you leave for the party, check to see if you have forgotten anything. Being prepared means looking forward to having a good time and remembering what you are supposed to bring:

*a birthday present,
food,
a game,
a guitar,
tapes,
or records.*

AT THE PARTY
Make an effort to speak to everyone.

Try not to have long, private conversations with your best friend.

Be willing to meet new people and make new friends.

Try not to occupy center stage unless you've been asked to entertain. Even if you are the class clown, give someone else a turn to be the life of the party.

Be willing to help with

*games,
refreshments,
introductions,
cleaning up accidents,
moving chairs or tables,
or
anything else that needs doing.*

AFTER THE PARTY IS OVER
If You're the Host:
Do say good-bye to every guest.
Do thank each person for coming and for anything special that person brought.
Do clean up the mess. If some of your friends stay to help, give them an extra "thank you" for that.

If You're the Guest:
Don't wear out your welcome. When the party is over, it's time to leave.
Do remember to say good-bye.
Do remember to thank your host and your host's parents, as well.
Do ask if you can help clean up.
Do be home before your curfew. This is a great way to make your parents happy.

*A successful party is one
   to remember
Whether it's April, June,
   or November.
When you plan ahead and
   do things right,
You'll have a party that's
   OUT OF SIGHT.*

6
Out on the Town

Part of the fun of growing up is getting to do new and different things away from home.

Informal things like
going to a ball game,
meeting a friend,
going to a school dance,
catching a flick,
enjoying a church social, and
eating out with family or friends.

More formal things like
attending a concert,
going to a ballet,
watching a live theater performance, and
eating out at a special restaurant.

Whether you're going out with a group or with one special friend, all the manners you have learned will come in handy at both informal and formal outings.

Informal Outings

Let's drop in on Gordon Murphy (you remember him . . . the kids used to call him "Grubbles") and see how he's doing these days.

Right now, Gordon and Melissa Rogers are leaving school together. They are on their way to Melissa's house to study for Friday's English test.

"How about stopping off at the Mile-High Cone Shoppe on the way home?" Gordon asks. "My treat."

57

"I'd love to, Gordie. But we'll have to hurry. I have to be home by four o'clock."

As they crossed the street, Gordon reached out and took Melissa's hand. "I don't want you to get hit by a car," he said with a grin.

At the ice cream shop, they both hesitated at the door. Suddenly Gordon remembered what he was supposed to do and pushed the door open, waiting for Melissa to go first.

She smiled at him. "Thanks, Gordie."

Gordon wondered why Melissa's smiles always made him feel weak in the knees.

A little later, at Melissa's house, Mrs. Rogers came into the den where Gordon and Melissa were studying.

"How's it going?" Mrs. Rogers asked.

Melissa sighed. "Pretty slow. We still have a lot to review."

"Maybe Gordon could stay for dinner," Mrs. Rogers suggested. "And you could study a little longer this evening."

"That sounds great!" Gordon exclaimed. "Is it OK if I use your phone? I need to check with my mom. She's expecting me home pretty soon."

By dinnertime, Gordon was starved, and the smells from the kitchen were driving him crazy. When he pulled out Melissa's chair for her, he hoped she couldn't hear his stomach growling.

Mrs. Rogers passed him a platter of fried chicken. "Help yourself, Gordon," she insisted.

Gordon started to do just that. He felt as if he could eat the whole thing, but he remembered just in time to take only a couple of small pieces. After the food had been passed around, he reached for his fork, then quickly put his hand in his lap. He had almost forgotten that Mrs. Rogers was supposed to take the first bite. When he was ready to leave later that evening, he remembered to say, "Thanks for the swell meal, Mrs. Rogers. That chicken was real-l-l-ly good!"

Mrs. Rogers smiled. "It's always nice to have you, Gordon."

As he went down the sidewalk and headed for home, Gordon couldn't help grinning. He had made a lot of points that day. He was sure glad he had bothered to learn some manners.

Gordon and Melissa did many things right. Read the story again, counting the number of times they remembered to be courteous and considerate. (Answers are at the end of this chapter.)

Out on the Town

GORDON AND MELISSA'S SCOREBOARD

1. _____
   _____
2. _____
   _____
3. _____
   _____
4. _____
   _____
5. _____
   _____
6. _____
   _____
7. _____
   _____
8. _____
   _____
9. _____
   _____
10. _____
    _____
11. _____
    _____
12. _____
    _____
13. _____
    _____

Gordon and Melissa didn't have to dress up for the informal things they were doing together. For informal outings, the clothes you wear to school are usually OK—as long as they are

clean,
mended,
and
appropriate for the occasion.

It's always better not to wear tank tops to dinner, shorts to a school dance, pants that are too tight, or see-through blouses.

More Formal Outings
Sooner or later, you will be asked to a more formal outing. This is when you should wear your best bib and tucker: coats and ties for boys, dressy dresses for girls ... and bring your very best manners to boot.

When Gordon's family decided to go out for pizza, he didn't have to worry about changing into his best clothes, but when they went to Pierre's for dinner on his mother's birthday, he was expected to dress up. He also had to practice a little **protocol** (PRO-tuh-call).

Protocol is a very particular way of doing things in special situations.

When Gordon's family arrived at Pierre's, they were seated by the **maitre d'** (headwaiter). It was the kind of place where Gordon pulled out the chair for his sister, Dodie, even though she was just a little kid.

60   *Out on the Town*

Gordon was a little shocked when a waiter opened his napkin for him and put it on his lap, but he didn't say a word, even though he was thinking, *Hey, man. Cut that out!* When the menu came, he was glad his father was there to explain it because there were many words Gordon had never seen before. He soon found out that:

Table d'hôte means a complete meal at a set price.
À la carte means that each item you order has a separate price.
Soup du jour means the soup of the day. On Pierre's French menu, soup was called **potage**.
À la king means with a cream sauce.
Au gratin means with cheese.
Florentine means with spinach.

His dad said it was OK to ask questions when you didn't understand the menu. Otherwise, you might get something you really didn't like.

"Boy!" Dodie whispered later. "I'm sure glad I found out that:

Escargots are snails,
Ris de veau are sweetbreads,
Grenouilles are frogs' legs,
Cervelle are brains,
and
Steak tartare is raw ground beef.

"I would have died," she moaned, "if I'd had to eat any of that stuff!"

"Those things are all OK to eat," said her mother, "but you shouldn't make the mistake of ordering something you don't want to eat."

After dinner, the whole family went to a concert together. Gordon felt pretty ritzy when an usher led them to their seats and gave them programs to read. *I wish Melissa could see me now,* he thought.

Partway through the performance, Dodie leaned over and whispered, "This is neat, Gordie, but how do I know when to clap?"

"You'd better wait and clap with everybody else," he answered. "That's what I'm gonna do."

"Gordie," she added, "I sure would like a drink of water."

"Sorry about that, Sis. You'll have to wait until intermission

The Right Way to Eat Spaghetti

like everybody else. Hey, Dodie, we'd better quit talking. People are starting to look at us."

Protocol is important at formal outings, but it doesn't prevent those outings from being lots of fun.

Dutch Treats

A few weeks later, when Gordon and Melissa were leaving school together, Gordon said, "I'd sure like to buy you some ice cream today, Mellie, but I'm a little short of cash."

"I am, too," Melissa sighed. "Hey, I have an idea. Why don't we go Dutch? You pay for your cone, and I'll pay for mine."

Dutch treating is often a good idea. It doesn't put one person on the spot to pay for everything. By Dutch treating in a tight $$$$ situation, you can share expenses as well as fun. It's OK to arrange to go Dutch when you go out on the town.

If you're meeting a friend
  or watching a game,
It makes no difference—
  it's just the same;

The way you act
  and the way you speak
Can make your day
  or even your week!

So wherever you go
  and whatever you do,
Don't save your good
  manners for only a few.

If you're wearing your best
  or duds you've just found,
Include your best manners
  when you're Out
on the Town.

GORDON AND MELISSA'S SCOREBOARD ANSWERS:

1. *Gordon:* invites Melissa for an ice cream.
2. *Melissa:* accepts politely.
3. *Melissa:* remembers her curfew.
4. *Gordon:* takes Melissa's hand in the street.
5. *Gordon:* opens door for Melissa.
6. *Melissa:* says, "Thank you."
7. *Gordon:* accepts dinner invitation politely.
8. *Gordon:* remembers curfew.
9. *Gordon:* remembers to ask permission.
10. *Gordon:* pulls out Melissa's chair.
11. *Gordon:* remembers to leave food for others.
12. *Gordon:* waits for Mrs. Rogers to begin eating.
13. *Gordon:* says, "Thank you."

7

Be My Guest

People have been visiting other people for as long as anyone can remember. Visiting probably began because human beings like to get together

to share food,
to share experiences,
to share ideas,
to share common interests,
to share news,
to share friendship,
or just to talk.

Sometimes people who visit each other are close neighbors. They can drop in for short visits because they don't have to travel far. You probably have many such friends.

Sometimes people who visit each other have to travel long distances. In the Middle Ages, taking a trip was difficult and tiring, and travelers had to stop along the way at guest houses where they could eat and sleep. These guest houses were called **hospitiums.** Can you see where the word **hospitality** comes from?

Having a Guest

Hospitality is important whether your guest comes from near or far. ALL guests should be treated with courtesy. You should make them feel comfortable. They should feel glad they came.

You can make guests feel at home by:

greeting *them with a smile,*

being *enthusiastic,*

showing *them where to wash up,*

showing *them where to put their belongings,*

offering *them refreshments,*

introducing *them to members of your family and anyone else they might not know, and*

locking up *any people-eating pets.*

When you are having company, whether for the afternoon, overnight, or even longer, it's your job to make sure your visitor has a good time and wants to come again.

Short, drop-in visits are easy. You don't have to plan very far ahead for these. Offering a cool, or warm, drink and a snack and showing guests where to wash up are all they will expect. If you want a visiting friend to stay for dinner, remember to ask a parent privately—never in front of your friend.

Longer visits take a little more effort on your part. There are extra things you should do to make houseguests glad they came. Look at the checklist below and find out all you need to know about becoming **The World's Greatest Host.**

HOW TO BE THE WORLD'S GREATEST HOST

1. Whenever possible, let your guest know when he or she is expected to arrive and how long the visit will be.

    "I'm glad you can come for the weekend, Bill. We'll expect you in time for dinner Friday night. I hope you can have lunch with us after church on Sunday before you have to leave."

2. Tell your guest what activities are planned and about any special clothing that might be needed.

    "Be sure to bring your swimsuit, Beth. We'll go to the beach on Saturday."

3. Find out if your guest has allergies to animals or foods.

    "Anne, do you still sneeze when you get close to cats?"

4. Try to find out if he or she has particular likes or dislikes, such as

    hating spinach,
    liking a window open at night,
    wanting an extra pillow,
    loving classical music, or
    resenting being called by a nickname.

5. Before your guest arrives, make room for your guest's clothes in a closet and a bureau drawer. Provide clothes hangers.

6. Check the bathroom. Make sure your guest has a private towel and washcloth, a fresh bar of soap, and a clean drinking glass. It is always a good idea to have a fresh toothbrush and

The Right Way to Eat Spaghetti

an extra tube of toothpaste on hand for emergencies.
7. Be at home when your guest arrives.
8. If this is your guest's first visit, show him or her around.

    "Come on, John. I'll give you the Grand Tour so you'll know where everything is."
9. Plan activities you think your guest will enjoy.

    "We have tickets for the ball game, Dave. You always said you wanted to see the Tigers play."
10. Explain the rules of the house and the family schedule.

    "Dad gets home by six o'clock and dinner is served at six-thirty. We can have a snack before going to bed."
11. Let your guest help with such chores as
    setting the table,
    feeding the dog,
    doing the dishes,
    or cleaning up clutter.
12. Don't overdo the entertainment. Give your guest some breathing time. Some people really like quiet moments when no one is "on stage."
13. When it's bedtime, call it a day. Don't take advantage of your friend's visit to beg for permission to stay up later.
14. Before you say good-bye, check to see that your guest is leaving nothing behind.
15. Be on the spot at departure time. Be sure to say, "Come again soon!"

Being a Guest
Being invited to someone's home is like receiving a compliment—like someone telling you, "You're a very special friend."

The way you act when you visit may determine whether or not you are invited again. Short, drop-in visits are easy if you:

Try to come at a convenient time. "I didn't know that you had chores to do, Bert. I'll come back later."

Know when to go home. "It's been fun, Jess, but I have to be home before dark."

If you came to study, don't goof around until after the work is done.

If you came to goof around, don't get carried away.

HOW TO BE THE WORLD'S GREATEST GUEST

Longer visits take a little more planning on your part. There are several things you can do to make your visit a success. The checklist below will help you remember the most important ones.

1. Make sure your host knows you are coming, when you will arrive, and when you have to leave.

    "Thanks for the invitation, Bob. Mom can bring me over about five o'clock on Friday. I wish I could stay for Sunday lunch, but I need to be home in time for Youth Sunday at our church."

    Unless it is understood that you are staying longer, your overnight visit should end before lunch the next day.

2. Ask your host if any special clothes are needed. Pack as lightly as you can. You won't need a steamer trunk unless you're going to Mozambique.

3. Bring essentials such as a comb, brush, shampoo, toothbrush and paste, and cosmetics—so you won't have to borrow personal items from your host.

4. Arrive on time and with a smile.

5. If you bring a gift for your friend or for your friend's parents, you can give it when you arrive. Gifts should be simple things such as

    a book,
    a loaf of fresh bread,
    salted nuts,
    fresh fruit from your garden,
    a bouquet of flowers,
    candy,
    a small plant,
    or anything else that is inexpensive, thoughtful, and considerate.

6. If no one tells you, ask about the family routine. Then follow it. Be enthusiastic about special activities. After all, your host has planned them for you. A good guest cooperates and never complains.

7. Respect the privacy of others. It's bad manners to snoop by opening drawers, looking into closets, reading private papers, sampling perfume or aftershave, or listening to private phone conversations.

8. Don't expect to be entertained all the time. When there's noth-

ing scheduled, it's perfectly all right to

*read a book or magazine,
watch TV (as long as you're not disturbing anyone),
take a short walk,
or
just kick back and do nothing.*

9. Make yourself at home, but don't overdo it. A good guest never:

   raids the refrigerator alone,

   turns up the TV or stereo,

   pounds on the piano,

   hogs the phone,

   takes a one-hour shower,

   drapes himself or herself over the sofa,

   strews personal items all over the bathroom.

10. Make your bed every morning and pick up all your personal debris.
11. Offer to help with meals. It doesn't take much time to peel a few potatoes, set the table, pour milk, or bring in the food.
12. Be on time for meals, and be dressed appropriately.
13. Offer to help clean up after meals.
14. When it's time to pack, collect your belongings. Make sure you aren't leaving anything behind.
15. Before you leave, say, "Thank you!" and tell your friend you had a great time. Make a special effort to tell a parent how much you appreciate his or her hospitality.

    "Thanks a lot, Mrs. Roberts. I really enjoyed myself. The skating party was super, and that apple pie you made was fabulous!"

P.S. Soon after your visit, it's nice to thank your host again by:

calling on the phone (if you live nearby) "Thanks again for the neat weekend, Joe. I hope you can come to my house next time."

or

writing a short note (if you live far away).

Dear Mrs. Roberts,

I really had a nice time last weekend. Thank you again for all the fun we had, especially the slumber party. I enjoyed seeing all my old friends again.

Sincerely,
Mary Beth Carlson

---

*If you're a visitor or a visitee,
It makes no difference; you can see
That the Golden Rule is where it begins:
"Give and take makes good friends."* —Scottish proverb

Be My Guest

8
Don't Call Me—
I'll Call You

Ding-a-ling! The telephone rang for the fifth time at the Butler house.

"Please answer the phone, Connie," Mrs. Butler said. "Can't you see I'm on a ladder, painting?"

"Get it! Somebody get the phone!" screamed Connie. "I just painted my fingernails."

Her younger brother, Eddie, charged out of his room, burned rubber all the way down the hall, took the stairs in four crashing leaps, and grabbed the phone in the middle of the sixth ring.

"I've got it!" he yelled into the mouthpiece. Then, in his best onstage voice, "Butlers' Pizza Parlor. We deliver."

Mrs. Butler shook her wet paintbrush at Eddie. "Haven't I told you to cut that out?"

"He can't help it, Mom. He's a little creep," Connie interrupted.

"Hey, you guys, I can't hear nuthin'. Keep it down, will ya, Connie?" Eddie turned back to the phone. "Who's this anyway? Oh, hello, Mr. Lingstrom. No, Dad's not home yet. Sorry."

He put the phone back on the cradle and headed for the front door, but his mother stopped him. "Just a minute, young man. Do you realize you hung up on your father's boss? That could have been an important call. If you're old enough to

71

answer the phone, you can learn to take a message."

Eddie shrugged. "It's all Connie's fault. If she didn't hog the phone all the time, maybe I'd get a little practice."

"I can't help it if I'm popular," Connie retorted. "And besides..."

"Besides nuthin'," Eddie grumbled. "All you do is yak about boys for hours at a time."

"Now stop it, you two," Mrs. Butler said. "You both need to learn telephone manners, and I think the time is *now.*"

Dial-with-Style
Alexander Graham Bell changed the world... and many parents wish he hadn't. **Teenage Telephonitis** is a well-known disease. Until now the only cure was cutting the wire. But this chapter offers a brand new remedy called dial-with-style. So, if your house sounds a little like the Butlers', you need to brush up on your telephone manners!

Turn the pages and find out all you need to know about practical, tested telephone techniques that teenagers can live with.

When You're Making a Call
1. **The world is at your fingertips** and it's a big responsibility. Your Aunt May in Maine may be only a digit or two away from Abdul's Tent Factory

The Right Way to Eat Spaghetti

in Istanbul. So be especially careful if you are allowed to call long distance.

Local calls should be dialed with care, too. Sloppy dialing will get you the wrong number and disturb the people at the other end of the line. **Hint for sloppy dialers:** imagine you are using a pay telephone and your quarter is in the slot.

Let the telephone ring long enough to be answered. Three times is not enough, and a dozen times is probably too much. Eight rings is right for most situations.

2. **What's in a name?** Everyone has one. Don't play guessing games with yours. Identify yourself at the beginning of the conversation. Never start with

"Guess who this is?"
"Hi! How ya doin'?"
or,
"Mom says I can come over at 5:00. OK?"

It's much better to say,

"Hi, Bill. This is Ernie!"
or,
"This is Connie Butler. May I please speak to Jill?"

3. **Making contact.** Always remember to ask to speak to someone. It's OK to say, "This is Liz Page. May I please speak to Connie?"

It's not OK to say,

"Hi! Is Connie home?"
"Hi there! Put Connie on the horn."

Don't Call Me—I'll Call You

or

"I wanna talk to Connie."

When you can't make contact because the person you want to talk to isn't in, you have two choices:

You can leave a message; "Will you tell Liz that Connie called and needs the English homework assignment?"

Or you can say: "Thanks. I'll call back later."

4. **Special Calls.** If you are calling about something important, be prepared. Take time to organize your thoughts. The best way is to make a list of the points you want to cover. Then, when the call is over, you won't have to dial right back again to say what you have forgotten.

When George called his science teacher about his project for the fair, for example, he said something like this: "Mr. Bigelow, this is George Owens. I'm calling about my science fair project, and I have four questions to ask. First of all, I need to know..."

5. **Wrong number!** Everyone makes an occasional boo-boo. When you dial the wrong number, don't panic, and don't hang up until you say, "I'm sorry. I must have dialed the wrong number."

It's always bad manners to ask, "What number is this?" or, "Who is this, anyway?"

When You're Receiving a Call

1. **How to answer the telephone.** Courteous people treat the telephone the same way they treat the doorbell. They simply go and answer it.

"Every time the phone rings, you act like you're in a drag race!" Connie Butler told her brother, Eddie.

Eddie gave her a dirty look. "Oh yeah? If I kicked back and waited for you to answer it, we'd all grow mold."

When the telephone rang at the beginning of this chapter, Connie was closest and should have made an effort to answer it, wet nails or not. Eddie didn't have to break a track record coming down the stairs, and when he got to the telephone he shouldn't have answered the way he did. Here are some of the things he could have said:

"Hello,"
"Hello. Eddie Butler speaking,"
or,
"Butler residence, Eddie speaking."

Eddie should forget about answers like

"Yeah?"
"Who is this?"
"It's your quarter. Shoot!"
or,
"Butlers' sanatorium. Ward B."

If the call is for you and you haven't already identified yourself, you can say,

"This is Connie,"
or,
"This is she."

But you should never say,

"This is her,"
or,
"This is me."

The Right Way to Eat Spaghetti

3. **If the call is for another person,** you can say, "Just a moment, please." Then set the receiver down carefully and go find the other person. Never scream, "Connie! It's for you!" into the mouthpiece.

4. **If the other person can't come to the telephone,** say so, but spare the caller the details.

5. **If the person being called is not home,** say so, then offer to take a message like: "I'm sorry, Mom's not here right now. Can I

Don't Call Me—I'll Call You

take a message for her?"

6. **When you take a message,** get it all, and get it right:

   —*Write down* the caller's name.
   —*Write down* a phone number, if necessary.
   —*Write down* the message.
   —*If you don't get the information straight* the first time, ask for a repeat. Don't be afraid to ask how to spell names and addresses.
   —*Repeat the message aloud* to be sure you didn't miss anything.

7. **Wrong numbers.** When someone has dialed your number by mistake, don't hang up, and don't try to be funny by saying things like, "Sorry, Barney doesn't live here anymore," when Barney never lived there at all. Instead say, "I'm sorry, you have the wrong number."

   If the caller asks, "Is this 555-9758?" it's OK to answer, "No, it isn't." But you should never say, "No, it isn't. This is 555-9785." It's not a good practice to give your correct telephone number to strangers.

The Sound of Your Voice

The sound of your voice is important. When you talk on the phone, people can't see you. Your voice is all there is, and you need to make the most of it. Here's how:

1. **Speak directly into the mouthpiece**—close to it, but not touching it with your mouth.
2. **Speak distinctly.** Don't mumble. Enunciate clearly. (You e-NUN-see-ate by pronouncing each syllable carefully.) Newscasters usually have good enunciation, and they are good examples of how to speak distinctly.
3. **Don't speak too fast.** Try to make every word count.
4. **Watch your volume.** Don't shout, but don't whisper, either. Just speak in a normal tone of voice.
5. **Remember,** the other person is forming a mental picture of you by the sound of your voice. Make it as pleasant as possible.

How to Quit When You're Ahead

Telephone conversations that seem to go on forever often go nowhere. You should never talk on the phone until you

get laryngitis,
develop telephone elbow,
or
get a cauliflower ear.

Respect whatever time limits your parents set. Use the kitchen timer, if necessary. After all, the family telephone is a convenience, not your private property.

The caller is the person who should usually end the conversation. The caller can end a conversation by saying something like: "Thanks for the homework assignment, Liz. I'd better get started now." But the person who answers the call can also be the first to say good-bye: "I'm sorry, Joe. I have to hang up now. Dad wants to use the phone."

Party Lines

If your telephone is on a party line (two or more families using the same circuit), there are special party line manners you should know about.

1. **Don't eavesdrop.** When you pick up the receiver and hear someone else already having a conversation, hang up immediately and quietly.
2. **If you have an emergency** and need to break in on a conversation, say, "Excuse me. This is an emergency. Will you please hang up?" It is against the law not to cooperate. It is also against the law to pretend there is an emergency.

Ten Telephone Tips for You

1. Don't make calls before 7:00 A.M. or after 9:00 P.M. . . . unless you have a real emergency.
2. Don't call friends during mealtimes.
3. Don't turn up the volume on the stereo, TV, or radio when someone else is talking on the phone.
4. Don't listen in on an extension line.
5. Don't **kibitz** (KIB-itz). A kibitzer is a person who stands around and offers unwanted advice.
6. Don't use a friend's phone without asking permission first. If it's a toll call, offer to pay.
7. Don't talk on the phone when your mouth is full.
8. Don't mess up the mouthpiece with things like:

   bubblegum,
   peanut butter,
   sticky fingers,
   or
   gear grease.

9. Keep it short. The Gettysburg Address has only 271 words.
10. "Phone as you would be phoned to!"—Bell Telephone System

9
On the Job

*Life is not
a having
and
a getting
but a being
and
a becoming.*
—Matthew Arnold

Joe groaned loudly and gave the lawn mower a push. "I'll never get this job done," he grumbled. "The grass is too tall and too thick." He cut a crooked path across the yard, then stopped and wiped his forehead with the back of his hand. "It's too hot to work," he muttered. "I'm going to sit in the shade until it cools off."

Down the street, Joe's friend, Keith, was having a different kind of problem. "You're grounded!" his father was saying. "You're not leaving this house until you write that paper for your English class. It was due last week, and you'd best get started right now, because nobody else is going to do it for you."

"It's dumb," Keith protested. "I don't see why I have to write about something I'm not interested in." He picked up his pencil and began doodling. Before long, he had a whole page of squiggles and swirls. He was admiring his work when the clock struck four times, and he remembered that he had planned to check out the new mall with Joe that afternoon. "What a way to spend a Saturday," he mumbled. Suddenly he picked up his pencil and threw it across the room.

BettyLu wasn't having a great Saturday, either. She picked up an armful of wrinkled clothes and dumped them in the middle of her unmade bed. "I don't see what the big problem is," she complained. "As long as I know where everything is, why should anyone else care what my room looks like?"

Joe, Keith, and BettyLu are each having an **attitude crisis.** Attitudes come from the inside. They are personal feelings. But they show up on the outside as clearly as our complexions. When Joe, Keith, and BettyLu grumble and gripe while working at chores, schoolwork, or part-time jobs, they don't get any medals for their trouble. But they do seem to

get tired faster,
lose their cool,
take longer to finish,
and
seldom get the job done right.

Let's take a look at your attitudes about work and find out how you really feel about the things you have to do. This **On the Job Quiz** will help you get your attitudes straight. Circle the answers that best describe your feelings. Be honest and work quickly. Don't go back and change any answers.

ON THE JOB QUIZ

1. I think my parents work because:
   a. it gives them something to do.
   b. everybody does it.
   c. they want to get ahead.
   d. they feel they have something to contribute. _____

2. A person gets paid for doing work because:
   a. work is tiring.
   b. everyone gets paid for doing work.
   c. the person likes working.
   d. the person earns his or her pay. _____

3. A job is:
   a. a drag.
   b. work.
   c. something I do because my parents make me.
   d. fulfilling. _____

4. What do I think about my first career job?
   a. My folks will take care of that for me.
   b. I'm too young to worry about stuff like that.
   c. I think I'll be an astronaut someday.
   d. I already have a job—school. _____

5. How do I feel about chores I do at home?
   a. My folks keep me busy so I won't have time for fun.
   b. I guess my parents are trying to teach me something.
   c. Chores are OK, but I get more than my share.
   d. Considering all my privileges, chores aren't bad. _____

6. When my folks give me a new chore to do, I:
   a. rant and rave until they say I don't have to do it.
   b. put it off as long as possible.
   c. do it as fast as I can and get it over with.
   d. look at each new responsibility as a challenge. _____

7. When I'm working, I:
   a. gripe to anybody who will listen.
   b. am angry with my parents for making me suffer.
   c. daydream about doing something else.
   d. think about how important the job is. _____

8. The purpose of chores is:
   a. to free parents from doing the dirty work.
   b. to keep kids off the street.
   c. to get things done so weekends will be free for fun.
   d. to share the labor so no one will be overworked. _____

9. When I have trouble doing a job, I:
    a. quit and do something pleasant instead.
    b. tell my parents or boss the work is too hard.
    c. try to get someone to help me do the dirty stuff.
    d. figure out what I'm doing to make the job hard. _____

10. How do I feel about getting dirty?
    a. Only pigs get dirt on their bodies.
    b. Only low-class people get dirt under their nails.
    c. It's OK if I am working on my bike.
    d. There's nothing like a hot shower after a dirty job. _____

11. What do I think about coming to work on time?
    a. No sweat. They can't get started without me.
    b. If I'm late, I'll say my alarm didn't go off.
    c. If I'm late, I could lose my job.
    d. If my boss wanted me to come later, he or she would say so. _____

12. When I have a problem in my job, I:
    a. avoid solving it and let someone else take the blame.
    b. do my best, but stay out of sight if I goof up.
    c. quit.
    d. ask my boss for help. _____

13. When I have a deadline on a homework assignment, I:
    a. get someone to do it for me.
    b. always turn it in late.
    c. wait until the day it is due, then panic.
    d. make a schedule and get it done early. _____

Score your quiz this way:

"A"—four points
"B"—three points
"C"—two points
"D"—one point

Now add up all your points.
Your total score is _____.

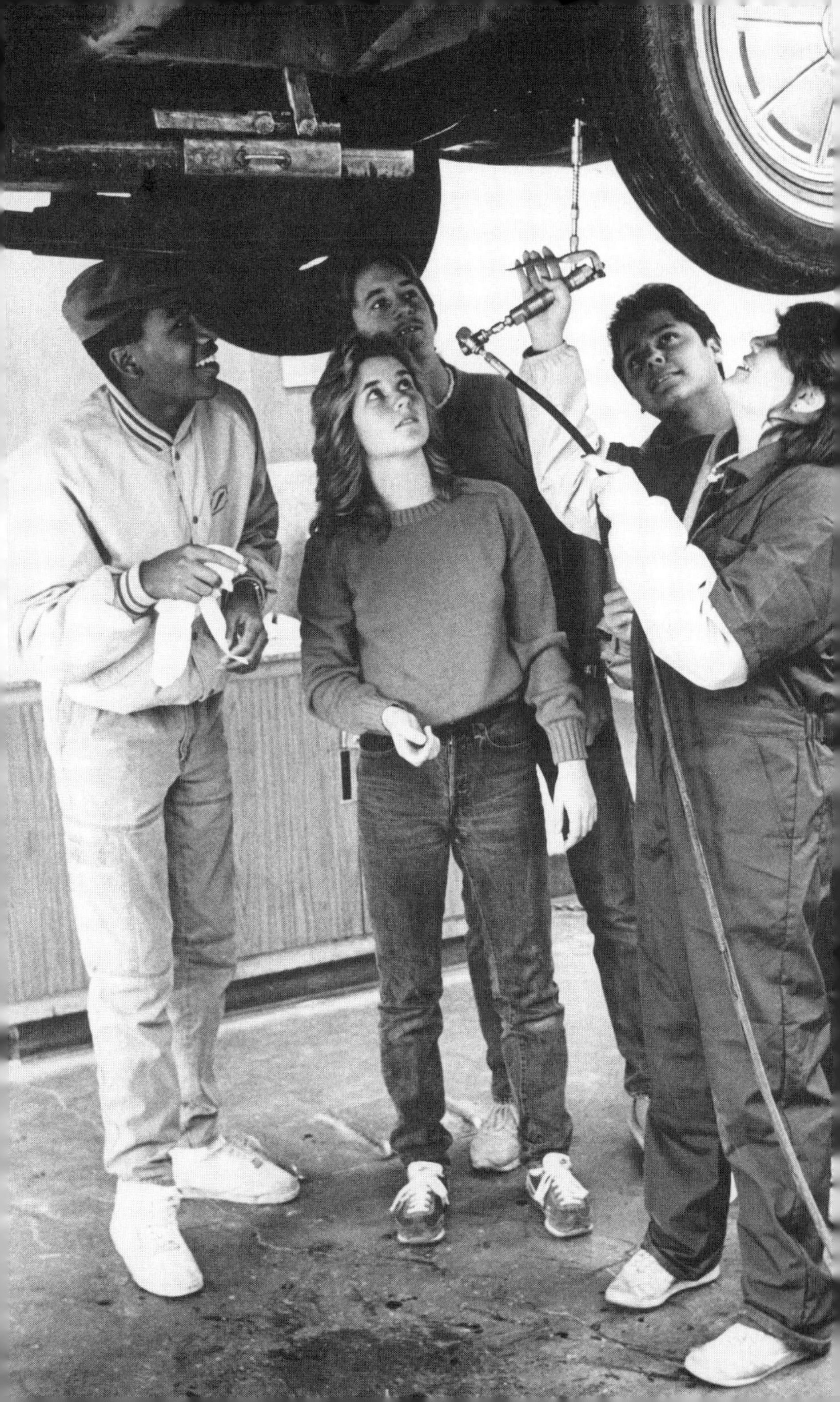

If you got between 42 and 52 points, you're having an attitude crisis. Maybe you never have had the chance to learn that working can be fun. Try tackling your next job with some enthusiasm. And remember—a sense of humor makes everything easier.

If your score was between 26 and 41, you know something about good work habits, but you are still learning. You need to be more sensitive to the feelings of others. Make a job well done your #1 objective.

If your score was between 14 and 25, your working attitudes are in good shape. Your job future is in the best of hands—YOURS!

If you scored 14 or below, you are too good to be true. Take the test again. This time, try to be really honest with yourself.

Don't worry if your score is disappointing. The **On the Job Quiz** is not a popularity test. It is designed to help you understand why kids like Joe, Keith, and BettyLu (and maybe you) sometimes have problems doing chores, finishing school assignments, or working for pay.

If you approach work and the people you work with in a positive, happy frame of mind, you'll feel better about your job—and you'll do better, too. A good attitude makes a big difference. Here are a few simple **On the Job Tips** that will help you in the very next job that comes your way.

On the Job Tips
—*Be on time*   —*Be courteous*
—*Be cheerful*   —*Be enthusiastic*
—*Be honest*   —*Be helpful*
—*Be efficient*   —*Be cooperative*
—*Be careful*   —*Be trustworthy*
—*Be considerate*   —*Be friendly*

Time flies when you're having fun.

—Old saying

10

Mail Call

> *Your letters
> are as good
> as a visit
> from somebody
> nice.*
> —D. H. Lawrence

Megan's best friend, Lori, was moving to another town. "I'll write," Megan promised, "and tell you all the news."

She did write, a couple of times. After that, she couldn't seem to think of anything to say except:

"How are you? I'm fine."
"It rained last night."
"I have a new English teacher."

Dullsville, Megan thought. Pretty soon the letters stopped.

Friendship Letters
Letters can keep long-distance friendships going, but only if they say more than, "How are you? I'm fine."

A letter is a good way to visit with a friend. You can keep in touch by writing letters that are fun to read and interesting, too. Here are some things you can write about:

Tell a long-distance friend how you feel. (Has something upset you? Are you in love again?)
Tell a long-distance friend about school. (Did something funny happen the first day?)
Tell a long-distance friend about news. (What's the latest scuttlebutt in your crowd?)
Tell a long-distance friend about

85

people. (Does Mr.
   Rogers still tell jokes
   in science class?)
Tell a long-distance friend
   about things. (Did you
   fix your bike? Get braces
   on your teeth?)
Tell a long-distance friend about
   your plans. (Are you taking a trip?
   Planning a party?)

   Make your letters sound like **you!** You can do this by writing the way you talk. Use your own words. Don't try to sound like a dictionary. Describe things the way you really see them, hear them, and feel about them.
   Here is the kind of friendship letter Megan could have written . . . and Lori would have enjoyed reading.

September 15, 19__ ← *feelings*

Dear Lori,
   I sure miss you, especially since school started. You should have been there the first day! Don Franklin slipped his pet snake into Miss Krump's top drawer. It was the first time I ever heard a teacher speaking German in an English class. } *school* } *people* ← *news*
   Betty's dad got transferred to Philadelphia, and Marge is going to a private school this year. It seems like everyone is leaving good old Eisenhower High. I feel as if I'm being deserted. } *people* } *feelings*
   Our whole family is going to visit my Aunt May for Thanksgiving. She lives in Porterville, remember? That's only a few miles from you. She says it's OK for you to come and stay overnight. I hope your folks will let you. Write and let me know! } *plans*

                                           Love,
                                              Megan

P.S. I finally got braces last week. ← *things*

---

86   *The Right Way to Eat Spaghetti*

Thank-You Notes for Gifts

Jason's Aunt Hilda sent him a wallet for his birthday. He really liked it and used it often. He meant to write and thank her, but he never seemed to get around to it. Then one day Jason received a note saying:

Dear Jason,

I'm sorry my birthday gift to you got lost in the mail. I'm sure I would have heard from you if you had received it.

Next week I'll go to the post office and put a tracer on it. Hope you had a nice birthday anyway.

Love,
Aunt Hilda

Getting a letter like that can be pretty embarrassing! Jason could have avoided a tough situation if he had written a simple thank-you note within a week after receiving his wallet.

Thank-you notes are not hard to write. Here are some suggestions that would have helped Jason, and might help you, too:

1. Be sure to **mention the gift.**
2. **Say you like it.**
3. **Say something extra** about it that shows you like it.
4. **Say thank you!**

Thank-you notes are generally informal, but they should still include things like:

your address,
the date,
the greeting,
the body of the letter,
the closing, and
your signature.

Here is the kind of thank-you note Jason could have written ... and Aunt Hilda would have appreciated.

---

412 Broadmoor Dr. ⟩ *your address*
Eastlake, CA 92346 ⟨
October 1, 19— ← *date*

Dear Aunt Hilda, ← *greeting*

Thanks a lot for the swell wallet. I really like it. How did you know my old one was in shreds? I especially like the hidden key pocket, but the nicest surprise was the five-dollar bill you tucked inside. ⟩ *body*

Thanks again. I hope you can visit us soon.

Love, ← *closing*
Jason ← *signature*

On the Job

Bread-and-Butter Letters

Herbie Snyder spent the weekend at his Cousin Ben's farm in the country. His Uncle Arthur took the boys fishing one day, and the next afternoon they visited the county fair. When Herbie got home, his mother asked, "Have you written a thank-you note to Uncle Arthur and Aunt Bea?"

"I already said thanks when I said good-bye," Herbie replied.

"That's not enough, Herbie. You need to write a bread-and-butter letter. It's not hard. Just tell them how neat it was, and try to remember some of the special things that were really fun."

Herbie groaned, but he got a paper and pen and began to write:

---

905 Franklin St.
Middleton, OH 40751
September 5, 19—

Dear Aunt Bea and Uncle Arthur,

I really enjoyed staying with you last weekend. The fish were sure biting, and they tasted great—especially with Aunt Bea's apple pie for dessert.

The county fair was the best ever. I'll never forget the look on Ben's face when his pig, Bonnie, won the blue ribbon.

Thanks again! I had a great time.

Love,
Herbie

A bread-and-butter letter says, "Thanks for having me as a guest." You can write one as easily as Herbie did. It's not hard, and it's a great deal of fun to remember a good time.

Business Letters

Everyone needs to know how to write a formal business letter. This is the type of letter you need to use if you are

asking for information,
making a request,
placing an order,
answering an ad,
or
applying for a job.

John was thumbing through the latest copy of *Boy Mechanics* when he noticed an offer for a free catalog of model airplane kits. There was no coupon to fill out so John knew he would have to write a letter. He was sure glad his mom had bought him a book entitled *The Right Way to Eat Spaghetti* because it told him what he needed to know.

Here's what John's letter looked like:

>
> heading {
> 1500 Maryknoll Drive
> La Jolla, CA 97750
> November 15, 19—
> }
>
> ↓ 4–6 spaces
>
> Mr. Robert Press
> Universal Catalog Company } inside address
> 555 South Vermont Avenue
> Los Angeles, CA 91111
>
> ↕ 2 spaces
> Dear Mr. Press: ← greeting
>
> ↕ 2 spaces
> I read your ad in the latest issue of *Boy Mechanics* about your
> model airplane kits. Please send me a copy of your free cata-
> log. Thank you very much.
>
> ↕ 2 spaces
> Sincerely, ← complimentary close
> *John Burke* ↕ 4 spaces
> John Burke ← typed signature / your own handwriting
>
> — body

John's letter is in a simplified form often used today. It has a **flush-left margin.** This means there are no paragraph indentations. Every line begins at the left-hand margin of the page, except for the heading at the top. If you have a printed letterhead that gives your address, you may write the date on the left margin, also.

John found out that business letters have six main parts:

The Heading,
The Inside Address,
The Greeting,
The Body of the Letter,
The Complimentary Close,
and
The Signature.

The Heading gives John's complete address and the date of the letter.

The Inside Address gives the name and complete address of the person John is writing to. The inside address should be exactly the same as the one used on the envelope.

The Greeting is a letter writer's way of saying, "Hello." John began his letter, "Dear Mr. Press." If you are writing to an adult, you should precede the person's name with Mr., Mrs., Miss, or any special title (such as Dr. or Rev.). If you don't know if a woman is a Miss or Mrs., you may use Ms., or you may simply use her full name without any title at all ("Dear Jennifer Smith").

Mail Call

If you are writing to a company and don't know what name to use, you may say, "Gentlemen," "Sirs," or "To Whom It May Concern."

The Body of the Letter contains your message. Try to keep your business letters short, simple, and to the point.

John's letter was only one paragraph long. If he had written more, he would have left one space between each paragraph.

The Complimentary Close is the way a letter writer says goodbye. John closed his business letter with "Sincerely." You might want to try using another closing, such as

Sincerely yours,
Yours truly,
Cordially yours,
or
Best regards.

The Signature should be handwritten below the **Complimentary Close.**

John remembered to enclose a **SASE (Self-Addressed Stamped Envelope)** with his request. It is always good manners to extend this courtesy when you are asking for something free.

Stationery

Formal business letters are best written on 8½-by-11-inch white paper, but informal personal notes can be written on almost any kind of paper as long as it is neat and clean. Boxed stationery is great if you have some. Used grocery bags are a poor choice, but lined notebook paper is OK if it's all you have to work with. (Remember to trim off any ragged edges.)

Once you begin, remember to **Leave margins** at top, bottom, and sides.
Write in ink, not with pencils or felt tip pens.
Spell correctly.
Keep the paper clean.

Envelopes

Envelopes should be clean and unused. They should be addressed

accurately
and
legibly.

Addressing Tips

Two addresses should appear on every envelope:
1. the address of the person sending the letter, and
2. the address of the person receiving the letter.

Betty Brown
1175 Main St.
Greenville, CA 92346

Mrs. Gladys Moore
509 Elm Road
Jackson, IL 60666

Words like *Street, Avenue, Drive, Boulevard,* and *Apartment* can be abbreviated like this:

St., Ave., Dr., Blvd., and Apt.

The **names of states** can be shortened if you use the official post office abbreviations. Two-letter abbreviations, such as CA (California) and FL (Florida), don't require periods.

Be sure to **include zip code** numbers. Put zip codes one space after the name of the state. Don't use a comma or period in between.

Don't forget to seal the envelope and put a stamp on it.

When the Kettle Boils ... It's Time to Let Off Steam

It's OK to write letters when you are angry. This is a good way to say what you think, and get it off your chest.

It's not OK to mail these letters if they say anything that can hurt another person. Never send an angry letter until several days after you write it. Take a good look at what you have written. Chances are you aren't even mad anymore.

Angry, hurtful letters should be sent to only one destination:

the waste basket!

Conclusion

*MANNERS
THAT MATTER—
AND A FEW
THAT DON'T*

Etiquette has come a long way since early cavemen used their fingers as eating tools. Over the years, long lists of dos and don'ts have been compiled, and hundreds of books about manners have been printed. Some of the earliest were called *Courtesy Books* and were full of rules for all occasions.

Most rules were based on reason. For example, men used to leave their hats on in the house. But when wigs came into fashion, men began taking off their hats indoors—not to be polite, but because the hats were too hot. After a while, people began to think of this practice as a sign of courtesy rather than an attempt to be comfortable. Today, men and boys are still expected to remove their hats indoors . . . even though they don't wear wigs!

"Don't spit in the fire!" became an important rule of health and good manners when people cooked their meals in pots hung above the flames of an open fireplace. Spitting in the fire—or any other place in the house—is still considered very bad manners.

Some old rules of behavior seem very strange to us today, but people paid a great deal of attention to them in days gone by. Here are a few to tickle your funnybone.

93

Some Old-Fashioned Manners

A Saturday night bath not only was considered necessary for good grooming, but was also made a law in Vermont.

A lady was not to show her bare elbows in public.

Good courtesy demanded that you should not kill fleas in the presence of others.

Sneezing at the dinner table or on a train was definitely taboo.

Only a nerd would gnaw corn from the cob. The kernels had to be scored with a knife, scraped onto a plate, and eaten with a fork.

Shoes for the street were to be high, warm, and neatly blackened.

Children were to be seen, but never heard.

Ladies were to refer to their "limbs," not their "legs."

A refined home was not considered complete without a canary.

It was crude behavior to wipe your mouth on the tablecloth or clean your fingernails with your fork.

Manners That Matter

Some rules of behavior change, but **Manners That Matter** never go out of style. It is always up to date to be considerate of other people.

You don't have to memorize a book of rules to be a well-mannered person, but you should remember to be

kind,
helpful,
polite,
good natured,
tolerant,
friendly,
dependable,
patient,
understanding,
and
giving.

"Treat others as you want them to treat you" (Luke 6:31, TLB), and you will have the kind of **Manners That Matter** all of the time.

The basis of good human behavior is kindness.
—Eleanor Roosevelt